PRAISE FOR *VULNERABLE FAITH*

"Using an array of examples that is both wide and deep, Jamie Arpin-Ricci draws us into a very deep place. This place of questions, trembling, fear, hope, faith, is at the heart of our vulnerability. It is in this very place that we most intimately find God and one another"

—Fran Rossi Szpylczyn
Catholic blogger, contributor to *Homilists for the Homeless*

"Jamie is an expert storyteller who with compassion and imagination seamlessly weaves together the old and the new, the saint and the sinner, the practical wisdom of the Twelve Steps with the timeless wisdom of the Scriptures. But his greatest feat in *Vulnerable Faith* is showing how transformative spirituality can be woven into the context of restorative community, where it belongs. Using the life of Saint Patrick as his guide, Jamie paves a way for all of us—on our own and in community—to approach a vulnerability worthy of our redemption. *Vulnerable Faith* is a primer on authentic community, a personal devotional book, and an insightful look into the human heart, all in one."

—Amy Hollingsworth
author of *The Simple Faith of Mister Rogers* and *Runaway Radical*

"Jamie Arpin-Ricci knows only too well that spiritual growth and transformation are the result of God's grace. I heartily recommend this book to anyone interested in teaching that has stood the test of time."

—Albert Haase, OFM
author of *Catching Fire, Becoming Flame: A Guide for Spiritual Transformation*

"Arpin-Ricci has found a unique way to blend the life struggles of St. Patrick to help us restore our own dilemma of neglected discipleship. Referencing the Twelve Steps model, the reality of Patrick's life, and the need for Christ in our own lives slowly unfolds into an understanding of how Christ fulfills shalom in all the areas of our lives. We all need this book."

—Randy Woodley
author of *Shalom and the Community of Creation: An Indigenous Vision*

"The artful retelling of the story of St. Patrick is done with imagination and care. Each chapter's installment of the story of the beloved saint is followed by theological reflection that probes and prods the reader toward holiness. This book is a fine resource for clergy, congregations, and missional communities."

—Elaine Heath
author of *We Were the Least of These*

"In this age of self-reliance and faux invincibility, the spiritual discipline of vulnerability is a rare thing indeed. Gently and yet provocatively, Jamie Arpin-Ricci uses the life and teaching of St. Patrick to show us that it is only through accepting our common weakness, our brokenness and our unequivocal need for grace that we can find the opportunity for fullness of life and true freedom."

—Michael Frost
author of *Incarnate*

"With creativity, skill, vulnerability, and insight Arpin-Ricci reintroduces readers to the risk of Christian faith, the hope of prophetic witness, and the true reward of costly grace for our time."

— Daniel P. Horan, OFM
author of *The Franciscan Heart of Thomas Merton*

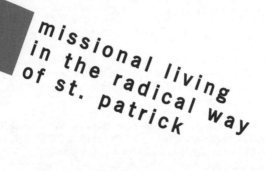

missional living
in the radical way
of st. patrick

vulnerable
FAITH

JAMIE ARPIN-RICCI

FOREWORD BY JEAN VANIER

PARACLETE PRESS
BREWSTER, MASSACHUSETTS

2015 First Printing

Vulnerable Faith: Missional Living in the Radical Way of St. Patrick

Copyright © 2015 by Jamie Arpin-Ricci

ISBN 978-1-61261-591-2

Library of Congress Cataloging-in-Publication Data

Arpin-Ricci, Jamie, 1977-
  Vulnerable faith : missional living in the radical way of St. Patrick / Jamie Arpin-Ricci ; foreword by Jean Vanier.
     pages cm
  Includes bibliographical references.
  ISBN 978-1-61261-591-2
  1. Patrick, Saint, 373?-463? 2. Christian saints—Ireland—Biography. 3. Martyrdom—Christianity. I. Title.
  BR1720.P26A77 2015
  242—dc23   2014047426

10 9 8 7 6 5 4 3 2 1

Published by Paraclete Press
Brewster, Massachusetts
www.paracletepress.com
Printed in the United States of America

To my best friend, partner, Kim.
Your love, patience, and support
allow me to be vulnerable.

CONTENTS

I shall give you a new heart, and put a new spirit in you; I shall remove the heart of stone from your bodies and give you a heart of flesh instead.

—*EZEKIEL 36:26*

The people in L'Arche with whom I have lived in community for over fifty years, men and women with intellectual disabilities, have taught me what it means to live vulnerably. For our greatest vulnerability is our need and longing to love and to be loved. And our fears of rejection, humiliation, and anguish solidify into hard walls, into compulsions and addictions, and even into hatred and the incapacity to meet those around us. Our fears turn our hearts to stone.

A heart of flesh is a heart that is vulnerable, one that is at risk of being wounded. But a heart of flesh is also capable of tenderness, a heart that can love.

This is the promise of transformation so beautifully illustrated in this book carefully titled *Vulnerable Faith*. The weaving together of the life of St. Patrick, the wisdom of Alcoholics Anonymous, and the real experiences of men and women offer a thorough and engaging orientation to what Etty Hillesum might call "coming to terms with life." Hillesum was a young Jewish woman living in Holland during the Second World War. As the war and the presence of Nazis in her town intensify, she shares an amazing journey of inner transformation and freedom.

> By "coming to terms with life" I mean: the reality of death has become a definite part of my life; my life has, so to speak, been extended by death.... It sounds paradoxical: by excluding death from our life, we cannot live a full life, and by admitting death into our life, we enlarge it and enrich it. (An Interrupted Life, p. 155).

Coming to terms with life means embracing the essence of our humanity, which is vulnerable. Life implies death. Loving one another implies the possibility of humiliation or rejection. This is reality. But to live in fear is not to live at all. And so we must be vulnerable so that we are free from fear, free to love.

Alcoholics Anonymous has always inspired me, too. It is also about freedom, by accepting vulnerability. It is a program that helps people to reveal the beauty that is within them. In a way, our life at L'Arche is similar. We are men and women with and without disabilities, living together to make known the value and gift of each person through our relationships with one another. Many of the people we welcome, the core-members*, have been terribly hurt, humiliated, rejected in big ways by being put into institutions, or in little ways by the looks of passersby that say, "You are weird," "You don't belong," "You are less important." They often have thickened layers of protection, which can be expressed in violence or depression, pushing away or closing up to those who try to become friends with them. Community building is also peace building, overcoming these barriers so that we can meet one another.

People that come to L'Arche to help often live the destabilizing realization that to meet one another implies a profound change in one's self. In the journey that community implies, the distinction between assistant and core-member becomes unimportant because we are all unique parts of one human body. Each of us is wounded. Each of us has been hurt in some way. Each of us has felt humiliation and rejection. And each of us has walls of protection that impede us from being in relationship with one another.

This book begins with a similar realization that the journey of recovery within AA is not unlike the journey of growth to sainthood and martyrdom, and is not unlike the journey of growth in love, for it is fundamentally a human journey. It begins with an acceptance of vulnerability and charts a growth in the faith that is needed to live this. It should never be said that "coming to terms with life," or community, or recovery, is easy. But it is essential if we are to live as children of God, as peacemakers, and with hearts open to loving.

---

* Core-members are the men and women with intellectual disabilities, truly at the core of our communities.

The urgency of the invitation to each of us in *Vulnerable Faith* cannot be ignored. In a world of terror and hatred, of protection and retaliation, it is a bold and important reminder to Christians of the radical nature of our witness as followers of Jesus. He is the Word made flesh, the vulnerable incarnation of God's love for each and every one of us. And it is in a relationship of mutual vulnerability with the One who loves us that we will be able to grow to freedom, that God's desire and our hope of shalom will be realized.

—JEAN VANIER

The virtues necessary to be a martyr are no different from the virtues necessary to be a faithful Christian.

—*CRAIG HOVEY*[1]

The disheveled and exhausted priest awoke from what little sleep he'd been able to cling to. Even at this early hour, sweat had begun to soak into his filthy striped prison clothes, promising another day of nearly unbearable heat in the confines of the prisoner bunker. Moving slowly, with the care and pains of a man twice his age, he got to his feet and stretched. As usual, he was the first one awake. He appreciated the few moments of silence each morning before he began his daily ritual of caring for the other men and serving their needs, from cleaning them of their own filth to administering the Eucharist. He took a deep breath and steadied himself for what was to come.

On this morning, however, the silence was different. Even with most of the other nine men condemned to starve to death in the bunker already dead, the silence was so complete, it was as if he was alone. Bending down on one knee beside the remaining, still human forms, he placed the back of his hand on each of their faces, their skin uncharacteristically cool in the growing heat of the summer day. He sighed heavily, slipped onto both knees, and quietly prayed for the last of his deceased companions.

His prayers were interrupted by the screeching protest of rusted hinges as the bunker door was opened, several armed guards stepping quickly inside, their rifles at the ready. As though the emaciated priest could have put up a fight, even if he had wanted do. *They are afraid*, thought the priest, *of me*. His heart filled with pity and compassion for his captors. He smiled kindly at them, hoping to ease their obvious anxiety.

"Wipe that smile off your face, prisoner!" Captain Fritzsch, the deputy commander of the concentration camp, barked as he stepped around the guards. This was the man who had condemned the men to die of starvation in order to deter other prisoners from attempting to escape. His cold pragmatism chilled the priest to the bone.

"It has been two weeks and you seem to be the last man alive. Characteristically stubborn and defiant, as usual," the captain sneered at the kneeling priest, who bowed his head and said nothing. "Do you think you have accomplished anything here? Do you think taking the place of one condemned man—who will die anyway—will give meaning to your life?" The deputy commander waited for a response, but again the priest said nothing.

"Very well," he added, "this bunker is needed for more important matters. Prisoner number 16770, I hereby sentence you to immediate execution. Bring the needle!" A camp doctor entered nervously, a readied syringe in his hand. Approaching the prisoner, he glanced back and forth between the priest and the captain, not sure how to proceed. Without a word, the priest raised his arm, offering it to the doctor, nodding to him with a look of such compassion that it was as though he was forgiving the man for what he was about to do.

This is how Father Maximilian Maria Kolbe, OFM, was martyred, giving his life to spare that of a Polish army sergeant, Franciszek Gajowniczek. Gajowniczek went on to live to the age of 94, seeing his family grow and expand over generations. He never failed to tell others of the heroic act of love that saved his life and the man who gave him his future, his life. On the 10th of October 1982, Pope John Paul II canonized Maximilian Maria Kolbe at St. Peter's Basilica in Vatican City to be remembered and venerated forever, a martyr for Christ.

WHAT A MARTYR REALLY IS

Few stories are more inspiring to Christians than those of martyrs—women and men who willingly, even joyfully, suffer and die for the sake of faithfulness in following Jesus. From the stoning of St. Stephen to the assassination of Archbishop Oscar Romero, church history is filled with example after example of this peaceful, yet unwavering witness of Christian love in face of suffering and death. We marvel at their courage and selflessness, revere their memories, and hold them up as examples of what it means to be followers of Jesus Christ.

Yet, despite our veneration of their faithful sacrifice and contrary to what we might say about their example to all Christians, all too often we view these men and women as so exceptionally holy that, while we can revere them, we are unable to practically follow their example. Whether we articulate it consciously or not, we view them through a lens of religious exceptionalism—the conviction that they are spiritually superior in ways that transcend the normal rules and expectations that come with living a human life today, therefore exempting us from the responsibility of even trying to follow their example.

For some, our failure to move past this is rooted in a genuine belief in our own mediocrity, even brokenness. Knowing ourselves like no one else could, we believe that we are far too flawed, afraid, lazy, timid, angry, jealous, or selfish to ever amount to anything more than the status quo of Christian faithfulness. For others, a feeling of resignation stems from an awareness of what true faithfulness would demand of us—the cost of true discipleship, which we, honest at least with ourselves, know we aren't willing to pay. In truth, both excuses are not so different or unrelated. Regardless, they produce the same result: a failure to embrace the calling of every believer to follow the way of the martyrs, the way of the Cross.

It is understandable why we balk from this responsibility, especially since the details of the martyrs' fates focus largely on the graphic realities of the suffering and deaths they experienced. I can say for myself that, apart from some significant transformation happening within me, it would seem unnatural (or at least unlikely) for me to respond to the prospect of such an end with eagerness, let alone joyful enthusiasm. Therefore, it is also easy to understand why we could misread the willingness of these saints as somehow demonstrating an absence of such fear as though it is a unique characteristic of their exceptional individuality.

However, when we explore the lives of the martyrs we see a pattern emerge. We begin to recognize in their stories, not an absence of fear, but a liberty from that very fear, just as present for them as for anyone. They somehow possess a freedom from the bondage of the fear of death that, by the Holy Spirit, empowers them to face martyrdom so heroically. As we discover the human persons within their hagiographies, with all the usual idiosyncrasies and imperfections of human experience, we are forced to admit that we cannot fairly hold them to a different standard than we hold ourselves. We are confronted with the invitation to participate in that same liberating transformation as fellow disciples of Christ.

This fundamental truth was echoed by Pope Francis:

> Both in the past and today, in many parts of the world there
> are martyrs, both men and women, who are imprisoned or
> killed for the sole reason of being Christian. But there is also
> the daily martyrdom, which does not result in death but is
> also a loss of life for Christ.[2]

In other words, the Church—the Body of Christ, every believer from
pope to postman to parent—shares in this "martyrological" vocation.
Pope Francis continues:

> Even though not every individual Christian will be killed,
> there is no way to distinguish those who will from those who
> will not. Even though not every Christian will be remem-
> bered as a martyr, every church that locates its identity in
> the cross is obligated to cultivate the virtues necessary to
> embrace all of its members to die for the cause of Christ.
> Every Christian is a member of a martyr-church.[3]

Yet, how do we "get there"? How do we become the kind of
people who embrace this transformation and step into the fearless
love of selfless service to God and neighbor? Again, we can look to the
lives of the saints, not only those who suffered a martyr's death, but all
who embraced this "daily martyrdom" in life. People like St. Thérèse
of Lisieux and her Little Way; Dorothy Day and Peter Maurin, whose
Catholic Worker movement continues to share life with those on the
margins even today; Kent Annan and John Engle who serve tirelessly
with Haiti Partners, facilitating educational transformation amid a

devastated nation; Mother Teresa and her Missionaries of Charity who selflessly pour out their lives among the world's forgotten and rejected; Mark Van Steenwyk and the Mennonite Worker community sharing life in Minneapolis's impoverished neighborhoods. In the lives of women and men such as these, we discover a work of transformation in hearts and lives—and this sort of transformation just might be accessible to us as well. Rooted in the fabric of Scripture and enlivened by the Spirit, it is a matter of following a journey with Christ that leads us from an isolated pretense of sin into Spirit-empowered communities of Christ. And with Christ, united as His Body together, we go about the work of seeing God's kingdom come on earth as it is in heaven.

It may sound easy when articulated in this way, but nothing could be further from the truth. Embracing the challenges surrounding such a faithfulness requires a lifetime, one that needs far more grace than discipline. Few things have been more intimidating in my life than having to sit down and write a book about this kind of vulnerable faith. After all, to have any credibility, people should really "practice what they preach." And no one is more familiar with my own inadequacies and failings than me. Yet, it is in the face of my own imperfection that the stories of the martyrs and heroes of the faith become all that much more hopeful for me.

THE CASE OF ST. PATRICK

Again, as we look at the lives of faithful servants of God, we see patterns. Their journey of transformation seems to follow a course that is reflected in the heart of Scripture. While this road of transformation can be seen in the lives of many individuals and communities throughout history, few have inspired me more than the life of St. Patrick, patron saint of Ireland.

From his selfish, carefree youth to his capture as a slave, we see Patrick's sinful pretense torn away, confronting him with the true emptiness of worldly pleasures and privileges. From the feelings of abandonment in enslavement, which led him finally to absolute surrender to God, to his miraculous liberation and return home, we see the power of hope and the promise of resurrection. Yet, most poignantly, it is in Patrick's return to the land of his captors as servant and missionary that the transformation of the Holy Spirit is best seen. Each of these points in his life illustrates a movement of grace that we will explore. At the beginning of the forthcoming chapters, we will glimpse these events in Patrick's life, as we did with Father Kolbe. While using the historical information we have, I will take some creative license (in areas such as dialogue) as I attempt to bring these stories to life in a more dynamic way.

Finally, while I promise that I will not give you "Five Easy Steps" to anything, there are steps that I will look to throughout the book. Namely, I draw deeply from the wisdom of the twelve-step program of Alcoholics Anonymous (often referred to as AA). The twelve steps explicitly parallel the process we explore in this book, fleshing them out in ways that are helpful. I will mention these parallels in the hope of demonstrating their wisdom. They are particularly helpful because they integrate guiding principles with concrete actions, refusing to let them be abstracted into mere ideals. Core to their process (and adapted for this context), the twelve steps involve admitting that we cannot control our brokenness; recognizing the need for God's intervention to give us strength; reflecting on all our failures, past and present, with the help of others; seeking reconciliation and making restitution whenever possible and beneficial; embracing a new life devoted to the principles learned; and compassionate reaching out to help others on the same journey. One could argue that these spiritual principles are necessary for everyone. Few movements reflect the kind of vulnerable faith we need like Alcoholics Anonymous.

Finally, I wanted to write this book because I believe with the German Lutheran pastor and theologian Dietrich Bonhoeffer that "cheap grace is the deadly enemy of our Church,"[4] in other words, a grace without price or cost, a grace taken for granted as though it is owed to us. Does anyone today doubt that the Church in the global north faces a crisis of this sort? Cheap faithfulness is taking the name of Christ as our identity without requiring the renunciation of self and selfish ends. It is seeking full intimacy with God yet giving little, if any, commitment. It is about negotiating terms with Jesus, as though we have anything at all to bring to the table. It is an abuse of love no better than trying to achieve the pleasures of intimacy by using another person for cheap sex.

So if you agree with Bonhoeffer, if you are intrigued by St. Patrick's journey, and if you see a need for transformation in your own life, this is your invitation to take some time to explore what greater faithfulness by the people of God—a more costly faithfulness, a risky and vulnerable faithfulness—might look like. It is a call to a life of devotion and a relationship of intimacy with the truest of Lovers (and through that Lover, with one another). It might be costly because that Lover asks for every part of our lives—mind, will, and emotions—body and soul. But in this faithfulness, from what I can tell, we may be able to find a true fullness of life and be an integral part of God's kingdom.

CHAPTER 1

A Word about Truth

I am the truth.

—*JESUS CHRIST*

For the twenty-plus years I have served as a missionary, most of the time has been in Canada, and then largely in our current neighborhood in Winnipeg. But I have also had the privilege to travel to many other nations. I've been to a densely populated shantytown near Kingston, Jamaica, and to the plazas of Madrid, Spain. I've participated in a banquet celebrating the end of Ramadan in a fine hotel in Morocco and enjoyed the unequalled hospitality of a Haitian family in a tin shed built alongside the rubble of their home, levelled by an earthquake. Married to an Australian, father to an adopted son from Ethiopia (and another on his way from Guyana), myself a dual citizen of both Canada and the United States, throughout my life I have been led to many places.

But there is one story I want to share with you now. As you read it, I want you to create in your mind's eye a picture of the events. I will intentionally share only the barest of facts, inviting you to fill in the blanks with your imagination. Here goes.

My wife and I were away from home and had arranged to meet with a Christian friend I'd known since childhood. When we arrived at the appointed place, my friend was late, so we waited for him to show. In time, he arrived, but to our surprise, he didn't come alone, but was joined by another young man who appeared to be about my age. As my friend introduced his companion, we learned that he was a Muslim. I greeted him with the only Arabic that I know, "As-salamu alaykum," and shook his hand. But within minutes of being introduced, I found myself lying face down, both men standing over me, their hands on my back. Anxiously, I waited for what they would do next. As my wife watched from a few feet away, each of them took a blade and cut into my back. To this day, I have the scars of that event.

None of what I've written of this event is untrue, and yet, I suspect, none of your reading has formed an accurate picture of what really happened. Let me fill in some other important factual details.

That day, my wife and I were in my childhood hometown of Rainy River, Canada. The friend I was meeting was a Christian from my home church who, along with his wife, used to lead my Sunday school class. He was also the town doctor. I was there that day to have two moles removed from my back. And the young Muslim man? He was a medical student working alongside our friend as part of his education. As my wife, Kim, sat and watched, with me anxious about the procedure, they indeed carefully removed those pesky moles, leaving the scars I bear to this day.

Now, I hope you are laughing, but I wouldn't be surprised if you feel a little bit deceived. Once, when I shared this story with a group of young adults, one young man looked at me with shock bordering on anger and declared, "You made me care about you, man!"

MOVING FROM TRUTH TO TRUTH

I intentionally left out details that resulted in giving you a very different picture of the events that happened. Not only did you likely get details wrong in your attempt to fill in the blanks of my tale, but in all likelihood, the scenario you imagined in no way bore much resemblance to actual events. You likely pictured the wrong setting, imagined the wrong emotions, and came to many false conclusions. That is not your fault at all. What other conclusion could you have come to? And yet, nothing I said in the original telling was false. Every piece of information I provided was perfectly factual. Is it my fault that you drew the wrong conclusions?

In fact, it is. This exercise illustrates how easy it is to send the wrong message. By simply focusing on the wrong information, by what we include and by what we exclude, we alter what people understand about what we share. We do not have to lie or intentionally mislead people in order for their understanding of our message to be very wrong. It is in this way that we see how facts don't always reflect the truth.

In the same way, we are responsible for the gospel we proclaim. Regardless of our own understandings of truth, it is all too easy to unintentionally represent the "facts" of the gospel in ways that can be as misleading. I suggest that this generally happens for two reasons: first, we fail to recognize that what we share, while rooted in our own understanding and experience with faith, can lack that same foundation—any foundation—in the hearts and minds of others. So what appears to be obvious or explicit to us can be strange and threatening to others. For example, the beauty of the Eucharist may have deep and powerful meaning for a committed Christian, yet without an understanding of the history, culture, and traditions of the Church, it wouldn't be surprising that others might hear our talk about partaking in the body and blood of our God as though we were celebrating some dark, cannibalistic ritual.

Second, misunderstandings happen because we have actually adopted ideas and beliefs that do not represent the truths of our faith. Our beliefs are so deeply intertwined with our cultures, languages, traditions, and even personal experiences that it can be hard, at times, to discern between core absolutes, contextual expressions, or outright distortions of the truth. Every believer, past and present, has made this mistake more than once. Unless we can claim that our beliefs are absolutely right and without fault (and I would question the honesty and maturity of anyone who made such a claim), we have to admit that we are probably wrong in some (probably several) details. So we pass those on to others, not intentionally, surely, but the impact of these dynamics shape the truth that people embrace.

This is why a lifelong embrace of the discipline of self-reflection, both as individuals and as communities—living in the dynamic tension between confident faith and the humble willingness to be corrected—is so critical. It is not that we should lack any certainty in what we believe, but rather embrace a sort of chastened certainty that embraces humility and knowing our own imperfection. This is critical, not only for ourselves, but for the sake of those who hear and see the gospel we preach and live. Consider the first of the twelve steps of Alcoholics Anonymous:

> We admitted we were powerless over alcohol—that our lives
> had become unmanageable.[5]

This foundational first step for the addict is critical and simple (though far from easy). This is where addicts admit the truth about how pervasively their addiction has impacted their lives. It is not about fixing it, explaining it, excusing it, or condemning it. This step is about exposing the pretense of having it together or under control and admitting how powerless they really are. As we can see from St. Patrick's own life, this wisdom is not reserved for just addicts, but provides an insight for all of us as to what we must do to begin our journey into freedom from fear and sin. This is the wisdom echoed in the Beatitudes, which promises: "Blessed are the poor in spirit, for theirs is the kingdom of heaven" (Matt. 5:3). While there are many implications to these profound words, those who heard these words would have immediately been reminded of texts from the Torah, and texts such as Psalm 34:4–6 and Zephaniah 3:12, where this language called them to humility and trust in God. Further, it would remind them that God esteems "him that is poor and of a contrite spirit" (Isa. 66:2, KJV). And it is only when we humble ourselves in confession and repentance of our sin that we can become heirs to the kingdom life that Jesus promises us.[6] Put simply, in the pop wisdom of TV's Dr. Phil, "You cannot change what you do not acknowledge."[7] We need to face and embrace the truth.

What is truth, after all? In John 14:6 Jesus said, "I am the way, and the truth, and the life. No one comes to the Father except through me." He didn't say that He knew the truth. He didn't say that He had the truth or even that He understood it. Jesus says that He is the truth. Jesus is the clearest revelation of God that we have, the embodiment in human form of all that is good and right, God-in-flesh. That Jesus took on human form and lived among us makes the Incarnation the most essential key to understanding the rest of Scripture and all of our faith. In this way, truth as we understand it is best expressed when it is embodied, incarnated, and lived out. Yes, we can learn about the truth. Indeed, we can share stories and ideas relating to that truth. Yet, the truest, most accurate expression of truth is what is embodied and lived.

For example, it is not the story of or ideas about Christ's work on the cross that saves us, but Jesus crucified. And so the call to Christians is to live out the faith, to embody it as fully and truly as is possible—more than we are called to ponder or debate ideas. Obviously, we are not God, so how can we be expected to live into that impossible standard? Because the impossible is made possible by the grace of God. Through the power and grace of Jesus Christ, we are ushered into the miraculous transformation that liberates us from the isolated bondage of sin and invites us into the Body of Christ. As we become more truly His Body, we are able to more fully live out the truth, because we live into the reality of Christ who is Himself the truth.

How do we get there? Surely it is not as easy as making a simple choice or flipping a spiritual switch. Instead, we have the opportunity to discover the practical means by which the often abstract concepts of "taking up our cross" and "sharing in His resurrection" become realities for us. Even when the means by which God accomplishes this transformation is beyond our comprehension, we do our part, one day at a time, one step at a time. It is hard work—not work that earns salvation, but hard work that reflects our loving response to the gift of a loving God.

What we are exploring in this book is not the definitive answer to what it means to be formed into the Body of Christ, but it is one way of seeing, understanding, and actively participating in the process of redemption and sanctification so that we can be Christ's agents of love and shalom to the nations. In other words, as we learn to embrace a vulnerable faith that freely brings our brokenness before God and others, we will become more like Jesus in how we live and love, both God and one another. And that love is what will help inaugurate the kingdom of God "on earth as it is in heaven" (Matt. 6:10). These are noble and high-minded words describing a mystical and beautiful work. Yet, it is work. It is hard.

The cross is an instrument of death, and to face it requires that we not only face our fears about death, but walk through them and willingly embrace death for the hope of new life.

WHY BROKENNESS IS GOOD FOR YOU

Several years ago, as I was teaching this material in our community, telling the story of St. Patrick and how each stage of his life followed this pattern of transformation, I was surprised by the people in our group who responded to it most strongly. One woman, a recovering alcoholic who had recently joined us, eagerly nodded her head, jotting down notes and sitting expectantly on the edge of her seat. Later, when I approached her and asked how she had found the material, she responded enthusiastically, "It's great! It's just like how I need to be working the steps in Alcoholics Anonymous." Not expecting such a response, I asked her to explain. Pulling out notes, she showed me a list of the key points in Patrick's journey, then listed the steps in order, running parallel with the chronology of his life. As though a light bulb went off, I began to see that the same process of transformation that God led Patrick on was reflected in the twelve steps.

Since that time, in our community we've intentionally begun to explore, experiment, and embrace the wisdom of the twelve steps as they add substance and practical wisdom to the pattern we see in St. Patrick's life.

Few things are more difficult to truly understand and embrace than the paradox of the Cross. After all, who can make sense of the notion that following Jesus is a death sentence that promises new life? What does it mean to "die to self"? How can death be, in any way, a victory? Nothing in our experience prepares us for the need to make such a counterintuitive choice, let alone every day, over and over again. Common sense teaches us that death means death, not life. Yet, the Christian community—the Church—must choose to move against the flow of the wisdom of the world to embrace the impossible foolishness of Christ. In other words, everything in us and most of those around us, perhaps even other Christians, will rail against such choices. But like the martyrs who knew that death has no victory over us, as we choose to follow Jesus, a resurrection beyond our imaginations awaits. For He is the truth, and only the truth can set you free.

CHAPTER 2

Our Nakedness

Let love be without hypocrisy.
—*ROMANS 12:9 (NASB)*

I t was late in the day when Calpurnius called for his horse to be saddled. He was preparing for his weekly ride through the town of Bannaventa, where he served as decurion. As a member of the town council, he took seriously his commitment to the people despite the unenviable responsibilities the role demanded. However, though he was a Briton, Calpurnius was a faithful citizen of ancient Rome and would fulfill those responsibilities without complaint, just as his father had before him. *Now, if only my son would show similar commitment.* Calpurnius sighed deeply at this thought. In fact, this very ride through the community would have happened in the much earlier hours had it not been for his wayward son who had already slept away most of the day.

"Patrick!" he shouted, his patience reaching its limits. He was on the verge of returning to the villa and dragging the teenager from his bed when the door swung open and the bleary-eyed, disheveled boy stumbled out, tucking his tunic into his breeches as he came. "Hurry up, boy. We've wasted half the day waiting for you."

"Many apologies, father," said Patrick with an easy grin. "Morning seems to have snuck up on me today." Calpurnius chuckled despite himself, taken in by his son's notorious charm. At sixteen he already seemed to have mastered the art of making people love him and was already popular throughout the region as a fun and generous young master, qualities that made them quick to forgive his idiosyncrasies. Yet, his father knew that such charisma would only take his son so far. Sooner or later the young man would have to grow up and put an end to his boyish ways.

"Morning? Midday and afternoon have also taken you by surprise! Never mind, let us just get on with it." The men mounted their horses and trotted out of the courtyard toward the village for their weekly inspection of the community and surrounding fields. The region, with its rich soil, was responsible for providing corn for many of the legions abroad, and Calpurnius liked to make sure everything was in working order for the sake of Rome. However, it was also important to him that the people knew and trusted him, which meant spending time among them. He took the role of caring for their welfare seriously.

"Father, is it really necessary for me to join you on these rides? Do you really need me to join you in chatting with the locals about the weather and their countless children? Think of all that could get done if I was freed from this task." Calpurnius did not immediately respond, mastering his temper and considering his words carefully before turning to his son.

"Oh, I am sure you could get plenty of gambling and drinking done between now and next sunrise, Patrick, but it is my hope that someday you will take my place as decurion here. In order to do that, you must know the land and its people. And they must know and trust you. To be sure, you are liked, but that is a far cry from being trusted. It falls to me to assess what our people need to continue to thrive, providing whatever I can to make that possible in a way that is fair and just. To be decurion, one must be a man of character and ethics."

"You are beginning to sound like grandfather," muttered Patrick. Calpurnius's anger flared at this.

"You'd be lucky to receive such a compliment as that! Your grandfather was a good and godly man, a presbyter in the Holy Church, and trusted by the entire community. The name Potitus is still spoken with respect and reverence among the people. We both have big shoes to fill. And the people will not always be so tolerant."

"Tolerant? I've heard no complaints. It's not my name that is synonymous with rigid rule-keeping and stern piety. You might have their respect, Father, but the people genuinely like me." Patrick regretted his words immediately upon seeing the look on his father's face, the sting they caused, yet he was tired of these endless lectures. They rode on in silence. Finally, his father pulled in the reins, stopping their mounts just outside the gates of the village.

"Is being liked so important to you, Patrick? And do the people even know who you are? If not, how can they truly like you? You have worked hard at becoming what you believe your friends want you to be. They call you generous, but what happens when the coin purse is empty? They declare that you are the life of every celebration, but what happens during times of crisis? If you would put half as much effort into being who you could truly become, rather than trying to be who you think everyone else wants you to be, you could become a man people would follow."

Patrick chuckled uncomfortably, trying to mask how deeply his father's words had reached past his facade. But his father wasn't listening to him anymore. Instead, he was staring off into the distance in the direction of the neighboring village. Patrick followed his gaze, at first not seeing what had captured Calpurnius's attention. When he did spot it, however, his heart froze in his chest: dark columns of smoke were rising thick in the distance, which could mean only one thing.

Raiders from across the sea.

BREAKING DOWN PRETENSES

To all who saw him, Patrick was the respectable successor to a legacy of a wealthy, privileged, and godly family. Yet, he played that role like an actor in a mask, pretending to be something he was not. Instead of being the upright son of local nobility, he was a selfish and arrogant youth concerned only with his own interests and pleasures. He presented himself as one thing when he was actually another. He was a hypocrite. This is, in fact, the very definition of hypocrisy, rooted in a Greek word referring to the masked performers playing fictitious roles in plays. What Patrick appeared to be to many was merely a false substitute for the truth. It was false, fake, a facade. It was pretense.

Pretense, like hypocrisy, is the act or appearance of being something that it is not. It is about giving the impression of something as being true that is, in fact, false. This sinful impulse is, perhaps, the oldest one known to humanity. After all, upon eating from the forbidden tree in the Garden of Eden, Adam and Eve immediately cover their nakedness, masking both their fear and shame. Hiding their true nature from God, each other, and even themselves, they sought to avoid the difficult dynamics of facing their sin and repenting. Instead, in addition to hiding their nakedness, they added to their pretense by attempting to shift the blame away from themselves—first Adam passing the buck onto Eve, who in turn pointed her finger at the serpent.

All of us are prone to this instinct toward pretense. It is ingrained in us as a way of thinking and acting that we are rarely aware of how often we present a false face to others. Sometimes it is little more than in the practice of expected social norms, where we respond to questions such as "How are you today?" with "I am doing just fine, thank you," regardless of how untrue that might actually be. Other times it goes deeper, where families who appear to be happy and healthy are, in truth, crippled with hidden addictions, shame, and abuse.

Take a moment to think of your deepest, darkest, most shameful secret—that thing you would be terrified to have revealed to your family and friends. Now imagine what it would feel like to have that exposed for all the world to see. What would you want to do in that moment of exposure? How would you feel? If you are anything like me (and anything like Adam and Eve), your impulse would be to run away and hide. Also like them, two feelings would likely surface: shame and fear. It is this shame and fear that keep so many of us locked into the bondage of pretense. While Genesis 2 says that prior to sinning they were naked and "not ashamed," in Genesis 3 we see that Adam confesses something more about the motivation to hide himself from God: "I heard the sound of you in the garden, and I was afraid, because I was naked; and I hid myself" (Gen. 3:10). It was also fear, not shame alone, that drove them to cover themselves and hide from God.

Shame and fear are powerful motivators. However, on closer inspection, we can also see how even shame falls under the category of fear. After all, what motivates us more to hide our hidden shame than the fear of what might happen if it were to be exposed? Fear of judgment. Fear of rejection. Fear of exclusion or expulsion. So, fear becomes a core seed of pretense, giving form to the lies that we tell others, God, and even ourselves—lies that beget more lies, each one another link in the chain of fear keeping us in bondage.

However, what is it that we ultimately fear? Hebrews 2:14–15 holds the answer to that very question when it says (speaking of Jesus):

> Since, therefore, the children share flesh and blood, he himself likewise shared the same things, so that through death he might destroy the one who has the power of death, that is, the devil, and free those who all their lives were held in slavery by *the fear of death*. (emphasis added)

These verses indicate that we are enslaved to the fear of death, a slavery from which Jesus has come to bring us liberty. The pretense of Patrick's respectability might not seem a response to a fear of death, but the very fear of judgment and rejection would have exposed the risks of the familial and social exclusion his sinfulness might result in. Richard Beck, Professor and Department Chair of Psychology at Abilene Christian University, helps us see the connection:

> As mortal creatures, separated from God's vivifying Spirit, humans are fearful and survival-driven animals, easily drawn into sinful and selfish practices. Because we are mortal and driven by self-preservation, our survival instincts make us tragically vulnerable to death anxiety— the desire to preserve our own existence above all else and at all costs.[8]

This fear of death is not only fear of immediate physical death: it can simply be the fear that our personae will be uncovered, "found out" for what they really are: fictions. Such fear is very real, contributing to our tendency to pretense, but also even toward violence and attempts to justify violence. It goes much deeper into our sense of well-being, materially, socially, and psychologically. After all, the fear of rejection from our families and/or communities threatens our overall sense of safety, stability, purpose, and even identity. We count on these things for our survival, both physically and socially. Without them, our ability to live and thrive is genuinely threatened. Thus, the fear of death lies at the heart of most of our sinful choices and our tendency toward pretense.[9] In other words, we fear death both physically and existentially.

THIS IS PAINFUL, FRIGHTENING WORK

While most of us will be primarily confronted by this existential death anxiety, I do not want to downplay the significance and reality of the threat of physical death. Years ago I received an e-mail from a young evangelical pastor who served in the rural American south. Having read something I'd written online, he felt that I would be a trustworthy and understanding person to talk about something he was afraid to share with anyone else in his life. Humbled, I invited him to be open with me, promising that whatever he shared would remain between us. Though he was married and the father of several children, he had come to realize that he was attracted to other men. He had no desire to leave his wife and family, but only wanted to make sense of what this meant for him.

Having walked many others through this kind of self-revelation, I was deeply sympathetic to the pain and confusion he was experiencing. As I had in other such situations, I asked him if there was anyone nearby whom he could trust with this information. What he said left me stunned. Without any sense of uncertainty, he told me that, should he share this information with anyone in his life, he would be in danger. He specifically said that if the elders in his church were to find out, he genuinely believed his life would be in danger. When I asked what he meant by that, assuming he was overstating things to make his point, he was quite clear: he feared that he would literally be beaten and possibly even killed.

Even his wife was not a safe person for him to share this with. In this case, his pretense was a necessity for literal survival. All I could do was try to help him from a distance. After a time, he abruptly stopped writing, and I have never learned what happened to him. Like this tortured young pastor, people all around the world are confronted with similar situations, where their survival is dependent on maintaining pretenses. It is important for us, who are less likely to face such circumstances, to remember these realities—not for the sake of being thankful for what we have, but to inspire in us a sense of justice that would desire to actively work for their freedom and security. We will explore this more in later chapters.

Perhaps the best-known description of the more common form of Christian pretense is aptly known as putting on our "Sunday best." Growing up in rural northwestern Ontario, Canada, attending a good, country church, we all knew that when you went to worship on Sunday morning you went looking your best: clean behind the ears, with freshly pressed clothing, and on our very best behavior. We would enter the church in our pristine condition, greeting one another with beatific smiles, and worshiping together as though Jesus had eradicated any sign of imperfection in our lives. However, we know this is not always a truthful representation of who we are or how we are doing. In truth, every one of us carries within the same fear that drives us into this very pretense, sometimes to the point that we believe if we can just put on a good enough performance, it might make it real. Our individual pretense becomes an unspoken social convention, a shared falsehood that allows us to remain together in relationship and community through the mutual acceptance of this unspoken untruth.

This is what psychiatrist and author M. Scott Peck called "pseudo-community":

> In pseudocommunity a group attempts to purchase community cheaply by pretense. It is not an evil, conscious pretense of deliberate black lies. Rather it is an unconscious, gentle process whereby people who want to be loving attempt to be so by telling little white lies, by withholding some of the truth about themselves and their feelings in order to avoid conflict. But it is still a pretense. It is an inviting but illegitimate short-cut to nowhere.[10]

Peck acknowledged the well-intentioned nature of this kind of pretense. It would be far too easy for us to dismiss this as something only others are subject to, seeing it as a dark, calculated effort to hide reality. In truth, while we all make such calculated choices more than we'd like to admit, the more fundamental dynamics of this reality play out unconsciously in ways we have accepted as normal. Then, blinded from the pretense in our lives, communities, and churches, we continue to perpetuate it.

It is not an all-or-nothing reality either. I'm not suggesting that we're all a bunch of dishonest posers. Most individuals and churches frequently demonstrate genuine authenticity and are seeking to live honestly, as did (and does) the church of my youth mentioned above. However, the presence of such authenticity on occasion does not exempt us from being subject to this trend in other ways. Again, this impulse goes back to the very beginning of the human story. No one is entirely free of it. Like Adam and Eve, we cover our nakedness in so many ways, motivated by the (understandable) fear of death as described above.

And it is not only our individual lives, families, or congregations who are subject to this kind of destructive pretense. In the same way, systems of governance, even in the larger church, are prone to behaviors such as cover-ups—again, often well intentioned—that not only rob the faithful of the opportunity of freedom from the bondage of their pretense, but also end up allowing (and perpetuating) abuses and injustices that go on to destroy lives. So we remain in the bondage of the fear of death. This fear touches every aspect of our lives. As we consider the Garden story, we recognize that the impact of sin touched what I refer to as the "four fundamental relationships" that God established: people's relationship with God, with each other, with themselves, and with creation. Each of these four relationships is unique.

First and foremost, fear and sin have disrupted our relationship with God. When they covered their nakedness and hid from God, the once direct, unhindered friendship that Adam and Eve enjoyed was broken and sullied. This relationship, upon which all other relationships are built, is most critically in need of restoration. God's intention at creation was for us to live in perfect, loving relationship with Him, created in His image, and made for one another. As sin brings fear and shame into our hearts, our response is to hide from God, covering our naked brokenness in any way we can in order to mitigate the consequences of our choices.

Second, beginning with Adam blaming Eve for the sin, our relationship with one another as people is broken. The otherness of Adam from Eve, from male to female, represents the otherness in all of humanity, in all of its variety. Where once that otherness was a reflection of the image of God in which we were created—the Trinitarian God, Three-in-One—now those differences divide us, making us adversaries threatened by our differences, motivated by selfishness and self-preservation.

Third, even the shame of their own nakedness sullied Adam and Eve's sense of self, with the image of God in which we are created being cracked as a result.[11] They were ashamed and covered their nakedness. Where once they were free to reveal themselves without fear or shame, now they are mortal, exposed and at risk, covering themselves to survive. In the same way, all too often we fear our truest selves would lead others to reject us, often justifiably so. Thus our sense of identity, our sense of self—our mind, will, and emotions, body and soul—is threatened, leading us to retreat into self-deluding pretense.

Even Adam and Eve's relationship to creation suffered from their sin, both in the blame-shifting onto the serpent and in the consequences for their sin (Gen. 3:17–19). The earth, which was once a free source of life, must now be toiled against to produce sustenance. Where animals once lived in harmony with humanity and each other, now they have become predator and prey. The intended integration of humanity with the rest of creation seen prior to sin reveals the truth that we were made for this world and this world for us. The physical substance of our bodies, the very air we breathe, and the earth upon which we live cannot be seen as separate from us, for without them we could not be. Yet, in the sinful and selfish choices we make, we further destroy that connection, killing our planet and ourselves in the process.

God, others, self, and creation—four fundamental relationships established at the beginning of time—were broken and remain broken today. It is in respect to each of these broken relationships that we see the formation of pretense borne of fear. And it is toward each of these four fundamental relationships that the restorative work of Jesus Christ is directed. As these dynamics worked in the transformation of St. Patrick, so too did they work themselves out in the transformation of the Irish people through Patrick's mission. The nature and breadth of his own redemptive transformation shaped the nature and breadth of the transformation of the Irish. Therefore, we can see how our own redemption impacts the mission of God in which we participate.

If we fail to address these broken relationships, the result in our lives is chaotic and unmanageable. Instead, as we were reminded by Bonhoeffer, we choose the cheap and easy substitutes for that which God has created us for and called us to. We all too often give up the chance for genuine peace, setting aside the necessary disciplines of humility and grace, and instead embrace the shallow substitutes of conflict avoidance and the denial (or exclusion) of differences.

On one hand, it could be as simple as buying into the pretense of the "Sunday best" mentality we spoke of earlier, where we ignore or dismiss conflict, forgiving wrongs in word, while holding on to the anger and resentment in our hearts. We present the socially acceptable, exterior image of peace, while anger and fear fester within, leaving us like white-washed tombs. On the other hand, we isolate ourselves from the complexities that inevitably arise wherever differences exist by embracing shallow generalities and defining our beliefs in immovable absolutes for which we demand unquestioning agreement. This is not to say that there is no absolute truth, but rather that we too often take false comfort by rejecting any notion of mystery or possibility of being wrong.

This tendency to see the world in terms of in-group and out-group is a common and insidious dynamic that comes out of these external judgments. All too often we define ourselves as much (or more) by what we are not and what we are against, as by who we are, what we affirm, and how we actually live. Having a clear, sharp line between who is in and who is out bolsters our sense of security in the face of our fear of death. While this might express itself in extreme ways such as blatantly hateful racism, we are very adept at framing it in such a way as to sanitize (even sanctify) it.

So it is here that we begin by acknowledging that pretense exists—the same pretense exposed by the first of the twelve steps. It exists in our lives, our families, our churches, and in the wider culture—pretense that is rooted in fear and that covers over our sinful choices, both those of action and inaction. In order to do this, we learn the disciplines of humility and honesty, choosing a different posture in the face of the hard questions we usually avoid. As we become aware of this tendency to dismiss and defend against these difficult questions, we learn to let go of the fear that threatens our sense of self and security, finding in those same questions the seeds of hope and liberty in Christ.

This process was powerfully illustrated recently as I was approached by a couple in our church, Alan and Beth, to help them walk through a crisis they were facing in their marriage. The crisis started when Alan made an inappropriate flirtation toward a single woman who was part of the community. When the young woman approached my wife and me for support and advice on what to do, we went to Alan, insisting that he needed to tell his wife what had happened. Needless to say, afraid of the outcome of such honesty, he pleaded with us to reconsider, insisting that he was truly sorry. While we were forgiving and understanding, we knew that he needed to tell Beth the truth. That is when he began to suggest that, if he was forced to do so, he would end his own life. Given his previous attempts at suicide in his youth, we did not take these threats lightly. But thankfully, after several intense days and sleepless nights, Alan confessed his indiscretion to Beth.

What emerged following this confession was that Alan had a long-standing pattern of this behavior in the past, a pattern Beth assumed had remained in the past. Yet, clearly he was still caught up in the temptation that fuelled that behavior. Beth was understandably crushed and needed a time of separation. Alan's adult children felt shocked and betrayed, as though they had never really known the man they called Dad. The church reeled, not only because of their friendships with the family, but also because the fallout deeply impacted the stability of the community's leadership, ministry, and growth. While shock and anger were there, everyone was also committed to Alan and Beth, believing that God could bring healing even in this unfortunate situation.

It's been difficult for some to see any silver lining in the situation. Yet, in the midst of it all, Alan was taking one small, significant step closer to freedom from the bondage of fear and shame. His family, while grieving the death of the perception they had of their father, could begin to get to know him honestly, both the good and the bad. He was given the opportunity to do difficult yet beautiful work living into this newfound vulnerability, choosing honesty rather than having circumstance thrust it upon him. The family was given the chance to develop deeper and truer relationships with each other, committing to being more authentic about who they were. And while the prospect of reconciliation for the marriage itself remained uncertain, both Alan and Beth chose to move forward committed to finding and embracing the best for themselves and each other, whether that is full restoration or loving release. There is more hope in honest brokenness than in the pretense of false wholeness.

Too often, our pretenses are exposed in moments of crisis like this. When we are caught in a sin and forced to take responsibility, the masks get ripped away. While difficult and painful, even this can be a form of grace, giving all involved the opportunity to see, name, and address the brokenness where it exists. It is a dynamic that does not just happen, but it is the result of a people formed by the grace of Jesus Christ extended to them in genuine expressions of transformation that must be chosen and participated in.

Again, Alcoholics Anonymous lends its wisdom to us in the second and third steps of the twelve-step program:

2. Came to believe that a power greater than ourselves could restore us to sanity.
3. Made a decision to turn our will and our lives over to the care of God as we understood Him.[12]

As long as we insist on trying to achieve our own freedom on our own terms, we are still buying into the lie of self-sufficiency that got us into the problem in the first place. We need help outside of ourselves. We resist doing this out of fear of giving up control, but it is not about control. It is about letting go in order to be helped. We need God—we need the Holy Spirit to transform us from the inside out. And, beautifully, it is in this process of restoration that we truly begin to see who God really is.

At the time of Patrick's abduction—the scene you are about to read—his worldview was fairly clear: he was a citizen of the Roman Empire, a member of the privileged class. While the locals were treated with respect, he understood himself to be their social better. But Patrick's tidy categories collapsed in the face of invading marauders, who would have barely ranked as human in his eyes, threatening the false stability of his pretentious classism. Suddenly, all his wealth, privilege, and education were emptied of their apparent power, leaving him to literally fight for his life. While such crises can do the same thing to our own pretensions, we can also take intentional steps to divest ourselves of these perspectives.

Young Patrick saw little incentive to challenge his privilege and the pretenses of his sin. As we will see, for him it would take a great tragedy to brutally destroy that pretense and reveal the hard truth to him. For far too many people, this kind of crisis is the only way these hard truths are exposed, rather than their doing so voluntarily. That makes sense. After all, why would we want to voluntarily expose our failings? They are painful, exposing us to shame and fear and the possibility of alienation, even exclusion from the security of our relationships. Why would we willingly embrace that kind of vulnerability? While such questions make sense, they pave the road to a dire destination. We do not need to wait to hit rock bottom in order to face and address our brokenness. It is into this very place—this scary place—that Jesus invites us so that we can embrace the blessing of the humble and contrite heart, if only we dare expose the pretense of our hidden nakedness.

CHAPTER 3

At the Cross

When we walk without the cross, when we build without the cross and when we proclaim Christ without the cross, we are not disciples of the Lord.

—POPE FRANCIS

W hen Patrick awoke, the world around him was cold and black, rocking unsteadily beneath him as though the earth itself had thrown off its moorings. Suddenly panicking that he had been blinded, he attempted to get his feet beneath him. Unable to move, he realized that he was bound, his arms behind his back and his ankles tightly together. However, he was able to turn enough to realize that he was not, in fact, blind, but that the sun had long since set. *How long have I been unconscious?*

As his head slowly cleared, Patrick began to understand where he was. The memory of the attack on his village, on his family, rushed back, again spurring him to another hopeless attempt to stand. This time, as his head slammed back down, he recognized the feeling of hard, wet wood. His mouth was filled with the taste of dirt, the metallic tang of his own blood, and... salt? He was bound in the bottom of a boat, which was cutting through the heavy waves under the cover of darkness. He had been captured.

He was a slave.

Slowly turning his head, he was able to make out the muscled forms of two of his captors, each plying through the water with the paddles in the bow of the boat, silhouetted by a bright, nearly full moon. If it was already this late into the night, Patrick knew the shores of his home were long behind him. With each stroke they were paddling away from his home, from his family, and from his life. With each stroke, what little sense of hope he might muster seemed to disappear with the swirling water that splashed steadily against the hull. *I am alone.*

This very thought, however, stopped him in his despair. Surely he would not be the only one captured. There must have been others, others who would be on this very boat. Carefully, so not to draw attention, Patrick lifted his head and turned it in the other direction. As he did, he found himself face-to-face with another captive, whose eyes were closed, a trickle of blood running from the corner of his thin-lipped mouth, his skin made even paler by the moonlight. He recognized the face instantly.

"Crispus!" he whispered, the shout of joy withheld in the last second. Relief overwhelmed his fear momentarily, and he felt deeply grateful at not being alone in the boat, even as he felt ashamed for at all wishing this fate on his friend. Patrick attempted to shift closer to his friend, whose eyes slowly fluttered open, struggling to focus.

"Patrick?" His voice was barely a whisper, less as a result of caution than because of his obvious weakness. A fresh line of blood trickled down his cheek.

"Where are we?" whispered Patrick. Crispus tried to respond, but choked by the blood in his throat, he was seized by a fierce bout of coughing. Blood sprayed from his mouth, splattering Patrick's face, who recoiled in disgust. Then, from behind his fitful friend, drawn by the coughing, one of the fierce raiders stood and approached the pair of prisoners. Patrick withdrew even further into himself as the man shouted at him threateningly in a tongue he did not understand. As Crispus's coughing fit continued, the man turned to him. Grabbing the struggling teen by the hair, he lifted him brutally from the floor until his chest was lifted clear and visible. A thick ribbon of blood slipped from a wound in his chest, pooling with the filthy sea water beneath him. The raider spat with frustrated disgust, shouting something to an unseen companion further astern. When he heard the reply, the savage grunted with resignation and bent over Crispus, who struggled to catch his breath. Seizing him by the belt, his other hand still firmly in the curly tangle of his hair, the brute lifted the weakened body of Patrick's friend over the edge of the boat. Crispus flailed weakly, his nails digging into the gunwale, but it was too late. The strength of the man and the momentum of his body won the battle, and young Crispus disappeared over the edge of the boat with barely a splash and was gone.

Here Patrick lay, captured and bound by savages from a wild land. Watching the dying body of his friend cast aside like little more than carrion, he could not help but wonder at the fate of his other friends. His family. Were they among those being dragged off to some unknown fate? Were they in this boat or another? Or were they bleeding corpses in the smoldering ruin of their village? Would he ever know? He could only hope they were alive. While he cared for them deeply, his hope was tied to the possibility that, if they were among the living, they would come for him. *They would come, wouldn't they?*

Would *he* come for them if the roles were reversed? Or would he presume them dead, like so many others? Even if he thought that they were alive, what would the chances be that he would be able to find them in such a vast and hostile wilderness? He shivered at the realization, knowing in that moment that in this situation he would mourn them as lost, rather than risk himself on such slim hope of rescue. Patrick hoped they were better men than he, willing to do for him what he was unlikely to do for them. And there was nothing he could do for himself. Neither his wealth nor his privilege meant a thing to his captors. His education was worthless in the face of a heathen people and their rough tongue. And his infamous charm, which he had always been able to use to get out of any situation, was mockingly useless now. His only worth to these people was as a slave to be exploited, that is, if he even survived the journey. If not, he was little more than useless weight to be cast aside without a second thought.

He was dead to everyone who once knew him. He was dead to the world he knew. He was dead, and yet this living death left him mercilessly alive to suffering the agony of the emptiness of what his life had now become.

STRIPPED NAKED

In the British crime drama *Broadchurch*, a tragic story unfolds about the brutal murder of a young boy in a quaint and quiet small town on the Dorset coast. With one of the lowest crime rates in England, where neighbors know neighbors by name and family roots go back generations, the community is rocked by this horrific crime and the ensuing investigation. This seemingly idyllic town is suddenly thrust under the magnifying glass of a sometimes brusque police detective who hunts for the killer, leaving no stone unturned. And the results are not pretty.

While the show is primarily a dark murder mystery, where the goal is to figure out "who done it" (a set of circumstances that few of us, gratefully, will ever have to experience), the subtext focuses on something far more mundane and frighteningly relatable. As police begin to investigate, asking questions of family, friends, and neighbors, all of the inevitable secrets, indiscretions, character flaws, and failings of the townsfolk get pulled to the surface. Regardless of whether or not the information has to do with the case, the relentless pursuit for the truth pulls the cover off every little lie and pretense of every person the investigation comes in contact with. The false stability of their apparently happy lives is torn away and left exposed. This is the kind of harsh exposure that Patrick experienced upon being kidnapped. His various pretenses vanished one by one, eventually leaving only a broken, helpless child at the mercy of those who cared nothing about him beyond his worth as a slave.

This is why I find *Broadchurch*, like Patrick's experiences, compelling. Though few (if any) of us have ever experienced a brutal kidnapping, most of us can easily identify with the people in that fictional town, as well as their secrets, for all of us live with our own layers of pretense. Like the characters in this television drama, should the light be shone as brightly and as closely upon us, we too would likely find ourselves thrust into the chaos of what it would expose. Patrick found himself in just such a place in the bottom of that boat.

When our pretense is exposed, whether by circumstances or by choice, what lies beneath is all the fear, shame, and uncertainty that we have worked so hard to deny, ignore, and conceal. M. Scott Peck aptly describes this experience as "chaos."[13] It can produce in us a deep sense of panic, a loss of control, spurring us on to attempt to restore order and stability, usually by retreating back into some form of pretense or another. After all, the appearance of stability feels much more preferable than the acknowledgment of the chaos that lies beneath the surface.

Unlike Patrick, we can usually choose to avoid such chaos, rationalizing it as "unproductive" and dismissing it. Rather than see the hard truth as an opportunity for grace, we convince ourselves that allowing this process to descend into chaos serves no good in the end. However, that very chaos is not simply an inconvenience to be tolerated, nor even an unfortunate by-product of the process to be avoided if possible, but an essential part of the process itself. Peck explains that chaos "does not simply go away as soon as the group becomes aware of it." Instead, by choosing to be resolutely present and unflinchingly honest about the chaos in which we find ourselves, as well as the impulses it produces within us, we encounter that grace. As Christians, we know this is the (somewhat paradoxical) gift of the Cross of Christ, where we are exposed—naked—having the illusions of our control removed from us, and where we are invited to share in His death.

When we strip away the layers of familiarity and religiosity, the story of the passion of Jesus is filled with chaos. Imagine: in addition to the trauma of seeing a man you dearly love and to whom you are deeply devoted about to be brutally executed, all the hopeful visions of a future that he represented, of God's established kingdom come to earth, would seem instantly destroyed. You would be powerless, torn between the desire to save Him, the will to die with Him, and the temptation to save yourself, even if it meant denying Him in word, deed, or the absence of either. Without the benefit of hindsight that Christ's resurrection is just days away, your world would be falling apart.

In the same way, our invitation to follow Christ is not a romantic, poetic platitude, but a genuine call to the chaos of the cross. It is, in many ways, a choice to accept willingly what circumstance thrust upon Patrick. While the cross most certainly represents death, in truth it is not so much embracing a new sentence to be inflicted on us, as much as it is the revelation of our existing slavery to death and the fear it produces. In other words, embracing this step does not simply *create* chaos, but *reveals* the chaos already in place, which we've hidden from others and ourselves behind the masks of pretense.

There is a brilliant scene in one of my favorite movies *The Big Kahuna*, where Phil (played by Danny DeVito), a seasoned marketing rep for an industrial lubricant company, is talking to his young, evangelical colleague, Bob (played by Peter Facinelli). Phil is explaining to Bob the nature of having character after an upsetting conflict:

Phil: The question is, do you have any character at all? And if you want my honest opinion, Bob, you do not. For the simple reason that you don't regret anything yet.

Bob: You're saying I won't have any character unless I do something I regret?

Phil: No, Bob. I'm saying you've already done plenty of things to regret. You just don't know what they are.

Whenever I am working through this topic of pretense and chaos with a group, people almost always push back in ways similar to Bob:

Group: You're saying that unless we create chaos, we won't go any further in this process?

Me: No. I am saying that the chaos is already there; you just can't see it yet.

In the same way, while Patrick did enjoy the temporary protection of his place and status, he quickly discovered that their power was empty in the face of certain enemies. In the face of almost-certain death and the destruction of his false security, Patrick, I can imagine, was pleading with his captors, willing to do almost anything to live and be free. In other words, the cross—the prospect of dying, both literally and existentially—confronts us with our fear of death, exposing our impulses to resist such an outcome by any means necessary. Again, the chaos is already there, born from the fear and shame that drives us to sinful and selfish choices.

It is important for us to see the connection between self-serving choices and the nature of sin itself. For most Christians, the belief held is that sin resulted in death. The inheritance we receive from Adam is our "sinful natures," and the punishment for that sin is, necessarily, death. "For the wages of sin is death" (Rom. 6:23) clearly demonstrates that the consequence for our sin is death. But that is only part of the story. This commonly quoted verse is only one side of a two-sided coin. When we read "the wages of sin is death," we understand it to mean that the painful consequence of our sin is death—but we should also consider 1 Corinthians 15:56, which reads: "The sting of death is sin," a seeming reversal of the previous verse. The meaning is also reversed, saying that the result of being subject to death is sin.

It is not difficult for us to understand how death is a consequence of sin, but it can be a real challenge for us to understand how sin is a product of our being subject to death. However, these two themes are intricately connected. Through sin, humanity becomes mortal, vulnerable to death. In the face of that threat of death, the impulse to survive—the impulse for self-preservation—becomes a fundamental source for our sinful choices. While we do not know for sure, it is not hard to imagine that Patrick might have been willing to compromise nearly anything for the chance of survival and freedom. In the same way, when confronted with not having enough, our fear can keep us from being generous to those in need, failing to trust in God's provision. I can think of many situations while growing up where, confronted with a fear of rejection or alienation from my Christian peers, I followed the crowd against my better judgment, even when it harmed others. Yet, despite this dynamic, we focus almost exclusively on the Romans 6:23 perspective, and not without consequences to our faith.

Richard Beck elaborates on this imbalance, pointing out that "an exclusive focus on sin tends to oversimplify the dynamics of our moral struggles" and that "by exposing the dynamics of 'the devil's work' in our lives, work produced by a 'slavery to the fear of death,' we will be better positioned to resist the satanic influences in our lives, better equipped to do battle with the principalities and powers of darkness, and better able to love as Christ loved us."[14]

Jesus places his focus not on our "sin nature" but on the self-sacrificial nature of love. In John 15:13 He says, "No one has greater love than this, to lay down one's life for one's friends." It would take many years for Patrick to discover this truth, but when he did, his love of God was greater than his fear of suffering and death. Then he was truly free to love—and not just love those who loved him, such as his family, but even (and especially) his enemies. On some level, family loyalty can be motivated by self-preservation, seeing our families as extensions of ourselves. While it is by no means sinful to care for our families, the point is that the love Jesus is pointing to is free of even those attachments, free to love wholly. And in order to truly love this way—to lay down our lives for our friends—we must be freed from the bondage of the fear of death.

This willingness to risk our lives as an expression of love is not limited to literally dying for others. It also includes our willingness to set aside our stability and security so that we are free to love those who most need it. This confronts our fear of death insofar as love includes giving from what we have out of our own limited resources. It can seem to be a threat to our own survival, as individuals, as families, and as church communities. First John 3:16–17 encourages in this respect:

> We know love by this, that he laid down his life for us—and we ought to lay down our lives for one another. How does God's love abide in anyone who has the world's goods and sees a brother or sister in need and yet refuses help?

The explicit meaning of "lay down our lives for another" is linked to giving to those who are in need. This is a love that is necessarily proven by how we actively relate to others, not just in words, as though love could be reduced to sentiments. Verse 18 goes on to remind: "Love, not in word or speech, but in truth and action." Again, truth is not just about words and ideas, but embodied love. This kind of active love is demanding on what we have—not only our time and energy, but our resources. Keep in mind, also, that this text was not written to wealthy, privileged believers, but a people who lived as subjugated members under the rule of empire. Such love is not conditional on our means or wealth. It is not surprising that our response to such a call to love inspires anxiety in us.

Christian hospitality, a central tenant of our faith that has waned in practice over the centuries, owes much of its demise to these very fears and impulses toward self-preservation. Early Christians, remaining true to the teachings of Christ and His Church, opened their homes and lives to "the least of these" because they believed that in so doing they were welcoming Christ. This sacrificial generosity and radical welcome of the other was legitimately risky and costly, requiring a great deal from those believers.

But the diminished tradition of hospitality owes its demise to this very fear. Sacrificial generosity and radical welcome of the stranger, the "least of these," are legitimately risky and costly commitments. And because these risks are real, oftentimes costing us beyond our means, giving anyway requires a liberty from fear that we often lack. So renown were early Christians for this kind of service to those in need that they were deemed a threat to Roman Emperor Julian, who had rejected Christianity in favor of Neoplatonic paganism. In a letter addressing his concerns, Julian denounces Christianity as atheism, complaining:

> Atheism [i.e., Christian faith] has been specially advanced through the loving service rendered to strangers, and through their care for the burial of the dead. It is a scandal that there is not a single Jew who is a beggar, and that the godless Galileans care not only for their own poor but for ours as well; while those who belong to us look in vain for the help that we should render them.[15]

Here we see that loving as Christ loved meant not only risking themselves by giving out of their limited resources to care for the poor—both their own and those outside of their community—but risking the wrath of the empire. They were truly living as witnesses for Christ, even and especially in the face of death. Again we see that freedom from the fear of death is central to our ability to be those very kinds of witnesses before a watching world.

The fear of death also manifests itself in our sense of social stability and acceptance. Patrick went from viewing the Irish as savage subhumans to suddenly being at their mercy, toppling the accepted assumptions about human status and worth. But loving like Jesus does threatens our place in many social contexts, as we have seen with the Empire's response to the early Christian witness. Galatians 1:10 says:

> Am I now seeking human approval, or God's approval? Or am I trying to please people? If I were still pleasing people, I would not be a servant of Christ.

True faithfulness as servants of Jesus Christ requires that we be free from the fear of rejection and alienation tied up with human approval. This is not to say that we demonstrate our faithfulness to God by trying to lose approval. Too many Christians justify their "righteousness" as being proven by how "the world" rejects them, when in fact they are rejected for legitimate things such as arrogance, being judgmental, and selfishness. Instead, as we seek to follow the example of our loving Savior, we can expect to meet with the disapproval of some, but our faithfulness is not to waver. This is possible, of course, only when we are free from the bondage of the fear of death.

A SEARCHING AND FEARLESS PERSONAL INVENTORY

In order to achieve that freedom, we learn how to identify those things that keep us locked in fear and face the ensuing (and necessary) chaos in appropriate ways. In order to see and recognize those dynamics, we commit to consistent and thorough self-examination and reflection. An excellent example of such a form of self-examination comes in step 4 of the AA twelve-step program:

Made a searching and fearless moral inventory of ourselves.[16]

This "fearless moral inventory" is one of the hardest, yet most essential steps toward recovery in the program.

As we will explore later, Patrick's years of captivity afforded him ample time for such unwavering self-reflection, leading to his eventual transformation. It is equally critical for our own freedom from the bondage of fear. Having admitted the pretenses that cover over our sin and brokenness, we cannot stay in the realm of generalities, but must name the specific choices we have made (and are making). We do this in order to recognize and admit the reality of where we are at and confront our excuses and rationalizations. Then, with the liberty that comes from the Spirit, we can begin to say, "Admitted to God, to ourselves, and to another human being the exact nature of our wrongs."[17] It is the very act of bringing these things into the light that furthers our freedom, resisting the impulse to creep back into the shadows of pretense.

This is not just about identifying our failings and faults. In addition to confessing our mistakes, this is also a time where, in the light of honesty, we begin to have the freedom to affirm that which is good and right in us. Honesty cuts both ways, including the positive, lest we fall into despair and self-loathing. It is also important to recognize and celebrate our successes, no matter how seemingly small, as we work together toward wholeness. This is why celebration is such a key part of AA's organizational culture. In fact, it can be good to start with the positive, which is a way of affirming the truth that fundamental to who we are as people is that we are loved by God. While there was likely little space for Patrick to celebrate the good in himself in the midst of his imprisonment, the refining process he experienced left behind the best that God had created and always intended him to be. The brokenness of sin is real, but it is the aberration, the anomaly, not the norm. This is a small way to remind ourselves that, even in the midst of the darkness, we are created in the image of God, and it is good.

Our natural impulse will be to resist this kind of vulnerability. Even once we've dedicated ourselves to doing it, we often subconsciously subvert the process by adopting half measures. For example, in making a list of our failings, we might list only those things that, while clearly unhealthy, are not so bad that we'd be completely embarrassed to admit them. So we get the affirmation of doing the hard work of honesty while holding back our most difficult secrets, sins, and struggles, keeping them locked up and away from prying eyes. This is nothing more than another form of pretense. And while we might learn to slowly be more open over time—not requiring people to jump from A to Z in one sweeping move—we should at least be aware that such a tendency to minimize and be selective in our confession is an impulse rooted in pretense. For the truth to set us free, we must be willing to, and actively working to reveal, the whole truth.

Clearly, we cannot be expected to remember every detail of every single sin in our lives. Even the "moral inventory" of AA understands these limitations. While we should try to be as open and detailed as possible in the process, the point is not about writing a rap sheet of every mistake we've ever made, but about helping us discern the root causes behind those choices. Members of AA are often encouraged to look at it through these five lenses:

Situational: What situations do I find myself in as a result of my sinful choices?

Behavioural: What specific behaviors do my choices lead me into?

Thinking: What irrational and unhealthy thoughts are being perpetuated?

Feelings: What unmanageable and unhealthy emotions are being stirred?

Core Mistaken Beliefs: What is the root of all of the above that lies at the heart of my sinful behavior?[18]

As we begin to do this, to see the heart of our brokenness and the sources for our bondage to the fear of death, we are able to glimpse the causes for our disconnect and the need for reconciliation in the four fundamental relationships. Those choices have kept us from living lives of honesty and authenticity, not only with others, but with God and with ourselves. This is why sharing our brokenness is so essential, because apart from it we are still relying on our own strength and capacity to find healing, which we have clearly seen we are not capable of doing.

Even Patrick was starkly honest about his own failings in his letter *Confessio*, read widely by millions since it was first penned. In our own ways, we must expose our nakedness before others confessionally and trust God and them to help us move toward wholeness. We must be willing to do this, even if we are not enthusiastic about doing so. After all, we are going to the cross.

THE CROSS OF CHRIST IS UNCOMFORTABLE

So we begin to come to terms with the paradox that we learn to face: there is nothing rational or natural about going to the cross. The cross is an instrument of death and suffering. Our desire to avoid it—and the ensuing chaos it inevitably exposes—is completely understand-able. Yet, we know this is what Jesus calls us to. It stands to reason, then, that choosing the cross must be an act of trust and faith, because our common sense will tell us to do otherwise. We will not always be able to trust our instincts, because they rely, not on faith, but on self-preservation. While those same impulses most often serve us well and can most often be trusted, in the process of redemption they can run counter to the path we are called to. Therefore, we rely on God (and the support of one another) to give us the strength to do the impossibly foolish act of dying to self.

There is comfort to be had: don't feel guilty or inadequate because you wish to avoid such suffering, chaos, and death. These feelings are not sinful but completely natural. Even Jesus, faced with His own imminent torture and death, prayed that the cup of suffering He faced might pass by. Yet, in the end, He said to the Father, "not my will but yours be done" (Lk. 22:42). Don't miss this: Jesus had a different will than the Father, yet was without sin. Why? Because He chose faith over self-preservation, even in the face of suffering and death. Don't let people question the integrity of your faith simply because you experience fear and uncertainty in the face of the cross you must carry. The loving response of fellow Christians is compassionate support, gentle grace, and the humble mutuality born of the knowledge that we have our own crosses to bear.

Therefore, if we are to face the chaos revealed at the cross, we must be equipped and prepared for what we will see there. One of the first things to happen when our pretense is stripped away from our relationships is that we are confronted with differences—differences in belief, experience, values, and priorities (to name a few). While before we might have given lip service to a unified commonality, more often than not we hold to it out of a desire to remain secure, accepted, and "right." Sometimes this is conscious, while other times we don't see our own dishonesty and inconsistency. I can say with confidence that anyone who has spent their life as part of a Christian church community knows that any apparent appearance of a perfectly unified body in all (or even most) things belies the levels of difference and disagreement that hide just below the surface.

The impulse to deny the differences and retreat back into an easy (or at least easier) dynamic of pretense is strong. In resisting this, it can seem logical to respond to the differences we discover between us as challenges to be resolved, problems to be fixed. Cloaked in the language of a well-intentioned desire to help—to convert and conform others to the better way (namely, *our way*)—we act out of our fear of the different. While this fear might manifest itself in more explicitly hostile expressions of rejection, more often than not we hide our fear and prejudice under the cover of something more acceptable. Yet, our desire to "normalize" our fear according to our own assumptions and beliefs is its own form of pretense, a false uniformity for its own sake.

All too often our underlying motivation is to restore things to a place where we are comfortable. Even with genuinely good intentions, how often are we motivated to comfort those who are weeping as much to end our own discomfort at seeing their suffering than actually for the sake of the sufferer? When people cry in public, they often resist strongly, then apologize when they cannot hold it back. Why? We all intrinsically know that our sorrow makes us vulnerable and others uncomfortable. Yet, Jesus calls us to another way: "Blessed are those who mourn, for they will be comforted" (Matt. 5:4). In the light of the differences and discomforts, we must choose simply to be present with them. We try to understand—not as a means to improve our arguments against their differences or discern a way to fix their problems—but to identify with them in whatever way we can and to acknowledge where we cannot.

This is easier said than done, because in acknowledging the differences and resisting the impulse to "normalize" the other, we are confronted with an alternative that always necessitates some change within ourselves. Our unchecked privilege, uncritically held beliefs, and even our sense of identity, having been built (at least in part) upon the foundations of pretense, must be questioned and dismantled. Such a shift threatens our sense of stability, stirring in us both that core anxiety and the impulse to resist that deconstruction, regardless of how necessary we believe it to be. The response to such a demand is usually fight or flight. For those who opt for the latter option of flight, it is most often away from the people and circumstances that created the tension and back into the very pretense they needed to escape from.

As for the impulse to fight, it is all too often as necessary as it is inevitable. To be clear, it is not that we need to pick fights in order to move through this process, but we can expose the hidden fear, anger, and chaos that is already there. Consider post-apartheid South Africa as they entered the gruelling and beautiful process of coming to terms with their horrific past and moving toward a better, more hopeful future. A commission was tasked with discovering the wrongdoings of both the state and the citizenry, in the hope of avoiding outright civil war and bringing about stability through restorative justice. Those who suffered were given a chance to voice what had happened—to tell their stories in their own words on their own terms—to have their truth validated and verified in the face of their oppressors. It also offered the opportunity for leniency for those perpetrators of the injustices who were willing to take genuine responsibility for their actions. It was called the Truth and Reconciliation Commission.

Note in the very name of the process, "Truth and Reconciliation," that prior to reconciliation is the necessity of truth. Unless we can speak the truth (and allow others to freely speak theirs) about both how we have sinned and been sinned against, we cannot hope to experience the reconciliation and redemption promised in the gospel. However, we must also recognize that the fighting that results in such honesty is not likely to be (or even intended to be) "productive." This stage is not about coming to a resolution of differences. It is about identifying and divesting ourselves of the right to demand satisfaction from others. It is about recognizing the illusion of our control and releasing it to the only one who has any claim on being right: Jesus Christ.

Interestingly, when groups begin this process, a subtle trend almost always emerges. People usually start sharing vulnerable truths about themselves by focusing on things from their past. This is to be expected and a good place to start. After all, our past choices make up who we are today. Many past experiences, especially those in our critical young years of development, set the stage for the rest of our lives. Further, because they lay that foundation, many of our current challenges are directly connected to those past events. This was especially clear in the case of the couple I mentioned earlier, where the husband had made inappropriate advances toward a young woman. For those of us who knew him, the husband's behavior was clearly linked to experiences from his past. Further, his wife revealed that these behaviors were a pattern throughout their marriage, a pattern she had forgiven him for time and time again. So when the new crisis emerged, the brokenness of their past became immediately relevant.

That said, it can be an easy, even unconscious temptation to focus on the brokenness of distantly past wounds and failings. While such honesty should include any wounds, including those from the past, they often have the benefit of having an impact without addressing the present reality. Our impulse will be to share things so far in the past that we receive sympathy from others without requiring much of us now. Where I get the most resistance is when I begin to ask the questions about people's current realities, especially their current relationships with the other people in the room. More often than not the critical differences and tensions that we most need to address are the present differences rooted in the everyday, mundane details of life and faith. Even the smallest offenses can take hold and grow roots of bitterness that go on to invade every other aspect of our lives, making it critical to learn the discipline of recognizing even the most seemingly unimportant differences among us.

Another common temptation falls to those who are leaders, whether by position or by merit of character and experience. Chaos goes against leaders' inclinations, for they are trained to create and maintain a productive and stable order for the people under their care and authority. Thus, in the face of emerging chaos, leaders will be tempted to "take charge" and manage the process. While there is a place for careful facilitation, more often than not such management becomes a gradual reversal into the pretense of organization. Organization is essential for the health of any community, but at this point in the process it works against the necessity of exposing the chaos essential to the cross.

LETTING GO OF OUTCOMES

There is also a challenge before all of us who feel we need a clear and positive outcome to any process. We believe that anything of value must result in a resolution that is beneficial to all. There is merit in those convictions. But it is our insistence to resolution *on our timeline* that is the problem. The chaos of the cross will lead us toward the redemptive resolution we all desire, but it will not be immediate.

No doubt St. Patrick would have insisted that he learned his lesson upon finding himself captured. However, the transformation that made him the saint we know took much longer. The chaos will feel much worse than the pretense we've emerged from, so our temptation is to question the value of such disorder and discomfort (questions that are often directed accusingly toward the leaders, thus furthering their temptation to control the process). And all of that without the immediate benefit of a resolution. Too often we rush to a resolution that, while having some merit, ultimately serves to ease our discomfort while avoiding the deeper transformation at work, leading us back into the pretense of false community.

Once, while teaching this material in a discipleship program for college-aged young adults, I planned to show them one of three movies to illustrate some of the principles we were exploring. I asked them to decide which of the three movies they thought they should watch, and said that they had to come to a full consensus in the group, not by voting, but through conversation, honesty, and vulnerability. What happened next was an hour and a half of pure chaos. The program leader approached me, asking if he could intervene, as the process "was going nowhere fast." "After all," he said, "it's just a movie!" While I encouraged him to let the process play itself out, he was right that the movie they picked, while important, wasn't the point of the exercise. However, what we all began to see in the process was that this group of people, who had been living and studying together for months, had settled into relationships fraught with pretense. Small offenses had become entrenched resentments. In-groups and out-groups had formed, leaving several people feeling unimportant. Theological differences had led to stubbornly closed minds and unwillingness to critically consider their own beliefs. And this task of simply picking a movie, without resorting to easy tactics, began the process of surfacing those differences. It was hard and it was messy and it was chaos, but the group came out the other side more of a community than when they started. One young woman commented, "Imagine how much more of an impact we could have if we practiced these things in more important decisions."

In the same way that immediate resolution is not available, since we must face and move through the chaos, neither is resolution immediately present at the other side of that chaos. Like the cross that Jesus died on, what followed was not immediate resurrection, but the cold, dark uncertainty of death, most poignantly expressed in His tomb. St. Patrick's own life nearly ended upon his capture, and yet it was not the end of his journey of transformation. What lay ahead for him was to face the emptiness of death and find within it the presence of God.

An Empty Tomb

People have a hard time letting go of their suffering.
Out of a fear of the unknown, they prefer suffering
that is familiar.

—THICH NHAT HANH

One would think that after years of exposure, a person would become at least somewhat accustomed to the merciless elements of cold, wild, and endless rain. Yet, all these years later, Patrick still ached to the bone as he sat on the hilltop, watching the flocks of sheep and goats whose value to his masters clearly far surpassed his own. Had it been years? In truth, he couldn't say for certain, though it felt like an eternity since his capture in Bannaventa.

Upon first arriving in the land of his heathen captors, Patrick was determined to escape. He refused to accept the indignity and suffering of a common slave. After all, he was a citizen of the Roman Empire, son of a decurion, and far too important and valuable to be wasted among these savages. When he found himself penned with dozens of other captured men from villages near his own, several began to form a plan to break out of their rough, wooden enclosure in the night and escape before anyone was the wiser.

When that fateful night arrived, Patrick was to be the last out of the cage. It was this fact alone that saved his life. Just as he was about to follow his fellow escapees, the men who had gone before him were discovered by a passing guard. As they screamed and fought back in useless protest, Patrick was able to duck quickly back into loosened bonds and feign sleep as the others were dragged away.

The next morning, Patrick and the remaining slaves were awoken by the shouts of their guards. The armed slavers came before them, dragging a man beaten almost beyond recognition. Almost. Patrick knew him as one of the other men who had tried to escape with him the night before. Where were the others? A tall, muscled man in a beard, who they had come to assume was the leader of their captors, stepped forward and began to talk to them in a threatening tone. While they could not understand a word of it, his intent was made clear: any attempt to escape would be met with unhesitating brutality. And should there be any doubt among the cowering slaves, the man drew his rough sword and, without so much as a hesitation, thrust it into the chest of the beaten escapee, his body crumpling before falling to the side, dead.

Something died inside Patrick that day. As the blade pierced the man's flesh, it was as though it cut into his own spirit, his own will to escape. He feared death too much to risk such an end. And so, with the dead obedience of one who has given up all hope, Patrick did not complain as they hammered the cold, cutting iron of his slave collar around his neck. And he did not resist as he was sold and taken deeper into the unknown wilderness to become the shepherd to some barbarian lord's flock.

Now, unknown years later, Patrick was a different man. Although he had given in to save his life, his impulse to resist persisted at first, but was slowly beaten out of him. He began to learn what it meant to care for the animals, learned the language and customs of his captors, and began to accept his portion in this new life. While it took a long time, he let go— not simply of his hope, but of his entitlement to be free. He was broken and empty, and in time, he began to let go of the last threads of his useless privilege and position, and simply became the slave shepherd Patrick.

In those moments of silence, when he truly let go, from within the emptiness in his heart came the distant and familiar voice of his grandfather. He began to remember the words of Scripture that Potitus had read to him as a child, explaining their meaning. And where once those words seemed a burden, if not a source of boredom, now they seemed to speak to his very soul. In that small, silent way, God began to fill the emptiness of Patrick's heart, and he began, after so many years, to pray. *Our Father, who art in heaven...*

A SORT OF NECESSARY EMPTINESS

In the weeks that followed Alan's confession to his wife and family, the couple decided they needed time apart. As sad as such a separation was for them (for all of us), it also brought a deep sense of relief for Beth. For too long she had done the lion's share of the work in the marriage, and it was time for Alan to be in a situation that required him to take more responsibility for his own brokenness. And she needed the distance to force that to happen, both so that it would require him to do it, and to protect her from her own habit of doing it for him. This is what she wanted. It was what she desperately needed. Moving to a local rooming house in the neighborhood, Alan dedicated himself to becoming whole again, with the hope of reconciliation as his prime motivator.

As the physical spaces her husband once filled with his presence and belongings started to empty, the reality of what was going on began to sink in for Beth. Without question the separation was a necessary step for her well-being—both of their well-beings, in fact—yet the emptiness around Beth began to fill her heart. She found herself second-guessing her decisions. Should she have insisted on Alan moving out? Should she have just kept supporting him and doing for him what he seemed unable or unwilling to do for himself? After all, didn't the Bible teach us to forgive "seventy times seven" times? Surely that would be easier and less painful than this.

These fair and natural questions are probably the result of the necessary emptiness that comes on the far side of the cross. Our impulse to retreat back into the familiarity of our brokenness, rather than face the uncertainty of the emptiness that precedes new life, can be overwhelming. That is because emptiness is a kind of dying, where everything that we placed our confidence in (even if it was often largely pretense) is stripped away. It can be terrifying and, thus, easy to justify avoiding. It takes a disciplined intentionality to embrace that uncertainty and take that step of faith into the tomb of emptiness. While some might argue that this emptiness was imposed on Patrick, the truth was that his place as a slave did not make him empty, but rather made a place for him to choose it. In the same way, we are given the choice.

It is like jumping out of a plane with a parachute, because people who skydive for the first time almost always experience extreme anxiety about stepping out into the nothingness of space, regardless of how confident they are in their equipment and training. Everything in their life experience up until that moment screams at them to stay where their feet are solidly planted and avoid falling from impossible heights. And yet, in that context, giving in to those legitimate anxieties actually works against you. In a similar way, by letting go of the expected norms and repeated patterns in her marriage, Beth was taking a step of freedom away from the destructive dysfunction, but the experience felt more like stepping out of a plane and free-falling toward earth. The deeper truth was that "the plane" of her marriage was on a crash course with a mountain anyway. Beth (and Alan) needed to choose to trust God, even when their only "parachute" was the promise that the God of the impossible would not let them be destroyed.

I understand this in my own life. I admit that there is a vast gap between intellectually acknowledging that I need to change and being genuinely willing to do what is necessary to change. This is where the wisdom of AA's sixth step confronts us, asking if we are "entirely ready to have God remove all these defects of character."[19] On one hand, asked if I am ready for God to remove all my character defects, of course I would say yes. To have all my defects removed by God sounds like a good deal. On the other hand, given the steps that preceded this one, I am also terrified by the prospect of what that will require of me. It is one thing to come to terms with having a deadly disease, for example, but quite another to willingly allow a doctor to amputate a limb in order to save the rest of the body. Even when we know that something is for our best, as we recognize the cost attached to that process—the chaos, fear, and uncertainty we will have to face—our impulse to resist rears its head quite powerfully.

It is only when we have come to the place where we are genuinely willing to make those choices and do the work that we can turn to God and "humbly ask Him to remove our shortcomings," as step 7 says. This is critical; otherwise, we might fall into magical thinking, as though God will supernaturally fix us before we are even willing to do the hard work ourselves. It is at this point that the rubber begins to hit the road, where we begin to see what is required of us to achieve the freedom we need. As members of AA are asked to start doing the hard work at this stage, it is not uncommon for them to refer to the first step: "First you tell me that I am powerless to change anything, but now you are asking me to do the work to change. Make up your mind!" While this can seem like a contradiction, it isn't. What we are called to is most assuredly an act of faith upon which we rely fully on God. That is not to say that we have to be perfectly willing, since doing this is sometimes like the desperate honesty of that father whose son was tormented, seeking Jesus's help, who cried: "I believe; help my unbelief!" (Mk. 9:24). Part of true faith is the paradox of hoping for the impossible in tension with our own uncertainty.

Consider the apostle Peter. Few stories of Peter are as memorable as the one in which Jesus, walking on water, approached the terrified disciples in their boat. Jesus defies all logic and common sense, calling Peter to come to Him out upon the water. No amount of practice, confidence, or willpower could equip Peter with the ability to defy physics and actually walk on water. This impossible invitation required nothing less than a divine intervention, for God to do for Peter what he could not do for himself—the impossible. Yet, Peter had to make the choice and take the physical steps to get out of the boat and walk toward Jesus. This is what it is all about: we must be willing to face the impossible, doing what is in our power to do, then trusting God (and/through others) to do for us what we cannot do for ourselves. Like Peter, we will make mistakes; we will sink back into bondage time and again. Also like Peter, Jesus will be there to reach out his hand and save us every time we call out. We must die to our self-sufficiency and trust in the impossible and immovable love of God.

In the same way, Patrick's enslavement was like a living death for him. Robbed of his wealth and privilege, he found himself forced to care for livestock—animals whose value to his captors surpassed even his own. Even the simple privilege of language—of being able to understand and communicate with others—was taken (at least until he learned the local tongue), furthering the dehumanization of his experience. While the dramatic and brutal intensity of his original kidnapping makes for a more engaging story, it is this seemingly endless and hopeless time as a subhuman slave, lost among the "savages" of a distant wilderness, that is far more akin to death. In that situation, few among us wouldn't give up.

Death, however, is the point of the tomb. When we consider the cross, we rightly view it as an instrument of death. It is the place where Jesus's life ended in suffering and pain. Yet, in truth, it is more accurate to cite the cross as the gate through which Jesus passed into death. After all, Jesus didn't simply die upon the cross, then leap back to life a few minutes later. His broken body was removed from the cross, prepared for burial, and left forever (they presumed) in the darkness of the tomb. He only remained there for three days, but it seems most of his friends and followers assumed that the tomb would be his body's final destination—a cold and dark stone cavern where he would decay alone, along with all their hopes for a new messianic age. In this way, the tomb captures the essence of emptiness in a way that even the cross cannot fully express.

COMING TO RECOGNIZE OUR EMPTINESS

I am reminded of the first Beatitude, "Blessed are the poor." Often it is the poor who recognize emptiness before the rest of us— and for obvious reasons. While I am not suggesting that poverty predisposes people to some form of righteousness, I have seen how their circumstances often free them from much of the pretense that our relative privilege affords us. So while the poor are not godlier on the basis of their poverty, they are often at least more authentic in their brokenness, and thus, perhaps, closer to honestly recognizing what true emptiness is. This places them one step closer to the hope of redemption and new life beyond the tomb.

Willingly embracing the emptiness of the tomb is more difficult for those of us in places of privilege. We have so much "stuff," so many activities and endless sources of distraction and busyness to fill any potential emptiness, that our pretense is better fortified against any attempts to expose it, whether through circumstance or intentionality. This is why, in part, Jesus speaks so strongly against the love of money. He did not demonize money itself, but recognized how easily we become enslaved to a different master, in bondage to mammon, instead of following Christ in loving service of God and others.

There is a scene in the 1999 film *Instinct*,[20] starring Cuba Gooding Jr. and Anthony Hopkins, that illustrates this point powerfully. We are introduced to anthropologist Ethan Powell (Hopkins) who has been living in the jungle with gorillas, missing for several years. When he is charged with injuring and killing several park rangers in defense of those same gorillas in Africa, he's returned to the United States and imprisoned until his state of mind can be assessed prior to trial. Enter Dr. Theo Caulder (Gooding), an ambitious young psychiatrist who hopes to make a name for himself by solving the mystery behind the brutal attacks.

While the rest of the movie is largely forgettable, the following scene has never left me, powerfully illustrating the raw honesty of the tomb.

During one of their private interviews, Dr. Powell expresses his disappointment with Dr. Caulder, at the young psychiatrist's failure to understand the truth behind what he did and why.

"I was wrong about you, *juha*," says Powell.

"Explain that," demands Caulder.

"Tell them to open this door. You're not the one, *juha*." [We learn later in the film that the word *juha* is Rwandan for *idiot*.]

"I'm not the one?"

"No."

"I'm not the one who cut your medication? I'm not the one to say you're competent for a hearing, a chance to get out of here? I'm the one, Ethan."

"Are you?"

"I'm the one."

"The one in control, huh?"

"Yes."

Without warning, Powell, having waited for the guards outside the cell to be adequately distracted, attacks the naively over-confident Dr. Caulder, taping his mouth shut. Pinning him to the table, the stronger older man puts the sharp end of a pencil to the young man's throat. He tells the terrified young doctor that he is going to give him a simple test; he lives if he passes, and dies if he fails.

Powell then asks the terrified Caulder what, in that moment, he has taken from him: "What have you lost?"

The captive doctor Caulder is given a paper and a crayon to write his answer. His first answer is scrawled, "CONTROL," which Powell immediate dismisses as wrong, tearing away the paper. Again he asks: "What have you lost? What did I take?"

The second answer is written: "MY FREEDOM." Again, the page is torn away, the answer wrong. Powell rants at the struggling man: "Did you think you were free? Where were you going at 2 o'clock today? Into the gym, right? In the morning, your wake-up call. In the middle of the night when you wake up sweating, with your heart pounding. What is it that has you all tied up, *juha*, tied up in little knots? Is it ambition? Yeah. You're no mystery to me, boy. l used to be you. Okay. One last chance… What have you lost? What did I take from you?"

And with his last chance, Dr. Caulder writes the answer that ultimately saves his life. Crying now, he writes: "MY ILLUSIONS."

"Yeah. Congratulations," says a smiling Powell, kissing the young man on the cheek as he rips the tape off his face "You're a student, after all. And you lost nothing but your illusions...and a little bit of skin."

What this scene beautiful demonstrates is that too many of the so-called freedoms we enjoy are mere illusions, pretenses covering over the truth that we are, in fact, enslaved to fear. Like St. Patrick, by being confronted with the fragility of life and his own mortality, Dr. Caulder's experience gave him the gift of clear sight to see through the pretense. It is our denial of death that predisposes us to pretense, while facing the inevitability of death offers us clarity and truth and, thus, freedom. The great hope in Christ and His resurrection (which we will explore in the next chapter) means that such a vision does not need to lead us into despair, but offers us a path to true liberty if we are willing to let go of our illusions and pretense and enter into the emptiness on the other side of the cross.

PERSONAL RESPONSIBILITY

Our impulse in the face of such a choice is too often one of (understandable) self-preservation. Thus our impulse to rush back into the false security of pretense—into the organization and power structures that we have constructed to isolate ourselves from our literal and existential mortality. Like our friend Beth, we might even be drawn back into the familiarity of our brokenness rather than face the difficult uncertainties and challenges of letting go. Patrick could have devoted himself to escaping rather than to facing the emptiness, but he refused. Like him, we can choose, step by small step, to enter into the process of emptiness in hope of new life on the other side. To their credit, Beth and Alan chose this latter path, the harder path, but the path that leads to life.

As we enter into this process in which we are confronted by our own selfish and sinful choices, born out of our bondage to the fear of death, one of the first impulses we will face (like Adam and Eve) is to mitigate our own culpability by shifting the blame (even if only by degrees) to circumstances or, more often, to other people. At times, we even blame God.

Learning to take responsibility has been one of the hardest things I've ever tried to do. While not excusing or ignoring the wrongs of others, especially those done against us as genuine injustices, in this process we should have as our primary commitment to recognize and take ownership for our own sin.

At Little Flowers Community, we have a saying, "My 100 percent is my 100 percent." In other words, personal responsibility is never mitigated by degrees. If I have sinned, no matter how small and no matter for what reason, I am responsible for all of that failing—that is my 100 percent. I cannot say things like, "I know what I did was wrong, but they did so much worse to me! They are at least 90 percent responsible for this conflict!" Even when this assessment is true on some level, the remaining 10 percent of responsibility is still my 100 percent and is the only thing I can know for a certainty I can deal with. This is not suggesting that justice shouldn't be pursued, but rather that in the process of finding liberty from our sins we must focus on the only thing we can control—our own heart. I often remind myself of this truth by speaking these words like a prayer: "The greatest sin in the whole world is that which is in my own heart."

But what does it mean to be empty? Growing up, I was warned by some Christian leaders that "emptying" was a New Age tactic that would clear my mind of God, leaving it open and exposed for exploitation—at best to false ideas and doubts, at worst to demonic possession. While these answers clearly reflect a bondage to fear themselves, there is at least an element of fair caution. We are not seeking emptiness as an end to itself, but as a means to an end. In order to appropriately understand this process of emptying and protecting ourselves against unhealthy understandings and practices, we need to understand the kind of emptiness Jesus both modeled and calls us to. I think we find that in Philippians 2:5–8:

> Let the same mind be in you that was in Christ Jesus, who, though he was in the form of God, did not regard equality with God as something to be exploited, but *emptied* himself, taking the form of a slave, being born in human likeness. And being found in human form, he humbled himself and became obedient to the point of death—even death on a cross. (emphasis added)

The word *emptied*, as used here, comes from the Greek verb form of the word *kenosis* (κένωσις). This idea of *kenosis* clearly marks the path that Christ has taken and called us to follow—a path of downward mobility, as it were, into servanthood and ultimate self-sacrifice. It is an emptiness born out of love for God and others and, as the following verses in Philippians 2 demonstrate, a humbleness that paradoxically leads to the exaltation and glory of God. Because Jesus embraced this emptiness and because it glorifies God, we can see that it is not a punitive emptying, but a meaningful and hopeful one, promising that something far greater will fill us.

While we are exploring this idea with the focus on our own pursuit of freedom, it would be a mistake to understand it as some sort of self-improvement method. In fact, it is the emptying of *self* that is the focus of *kenosis*, exactly what is meant in Matthew 16:24–26 when Jesus said:

> If any want to become my followers, let them deny them-
> selves and take up their cross and follow me. For those who
> want to save their life will lose it, and those who lose their
> life for my sake will find it. For what will it profit them if they
> gain the whole world but forfeit their life? Or what will they
> give in return for their life?

This is what Richard Beck calls developing an "eccentric identity."[21] He is not referring to an eccentricity of personality—that is, being unconventional or strange—but a more technical meaning of *eccentric*: "an identity grounded *outside* the boundary of the self."[22] Again, the direction that this journey is leading us on is one oriented to the north star of love. Beck continues:

> Following the example of Jesus, we become "nothing."
> In a sense, we "die"—and thus we no longer have to fear

dispossession, loss, diminishment, or expenditure in the face of death. Not that we seek out such losses. But we form our identities in such a way that we are freed from the anxiety of self-preservation, which makes different choices and modes of being human open and available to us. The creation of a secure heart makes love a possibility. It enables us to do something that biological creatures worried about self-preservation don't naturally do: place the interests of others before our own.[23]

Such a commitment to selfless love—of eccentric identity—is one that requires a lifetime commitment of practiced disciplines. Few of us will find ourselves in captivity like Patrick, affording the opportunity to make emptiness our only focus. Instead, most of us have to learn to recognize and name our feelings, assumptions, ideas, motives, and fears. Not denying them, but identifying them, refusing to allow them to be our central point of reference for self and others. If we fail to, they become barriers to genuinely understanding one another and effectively communicating. Just as my editor and friend posted on Facebook this morning, "Do you ever feel like everyone writes, and no one reads?" so it is easy to feel like everyone is fighting to have their voice heard—their perspective affirmed, needs met, desires satiated—but few are listening to hear the voices of others. Few are willing to learn from the other. Few are seeking to meet the needs of the least of these. And too few of us are learning to deny ourselves and follow Christ. *Kenosis* calls us to empty ourselves of the self-serving voices and hear the voice of God (and the voices of others) first and foremost.

This is a paradoxical promise. As we enter into loving service of others, and they extend that same gift to us, we will not need to advocate for ourselves as much, but can focus on serving others, trusting they will do the same for us. And it is an act of trust because it won't always work out that way. After all, what if I trust others to care for my needs, giving myself in the service of others, but then they fail to support me? Should we wait for some guarantee before putting ourselves out there?

No. Remember that Jesus embraced this emptiness, even when it led to His suffering and death—"while we were still sinners." While we can learn to better discern healthy and careful ways to appropriately care for ourselves, there is no clear and easy directive that shows us how to navigate the tension. The promise of this process we are engaging is that God will transform us together into His people, into community. And in community, such trust comes (relatively) easier. We are called to trust as a means to produce that community. It is a risk. And given the choice, we are called to err on the side of sacrifice.

SPIRITUAL DISCIPLINES

As we try to live out this paradox in our lives, we are well served in learning the disciplines of peace, both internal and relational. Practices such as meditation and reflection are so important. The capacity to quiet our hearts and minds is essential to the process of self-emptiness because those voices that need silencing most often reveal the very places where our fears and uncertainties lie, and because it is in that quietness that we begin to learn how to truly hear, both God and others. While we won't explore this theme in detail here, history is rich with examples of traditions where such meditation is significant. Perhaps the best example is *The Spiritual Exercises of St. Ignatius of Loyola*, the founder of the Jesuits. The depth and beauty of the exercises have led to their use among Christians of various traditions, clergy and laity. If you are not familiar with them, I highly recommend exploring them.

While the disciplines of meditation are often primarily internal, they provide us with the necessary emptiness and eccentric focus to truly listen to others. As we work to develop the external disciplines of peace and peacemaking, the firm foundation found in meditation is essential.

We must then also develop disciplines such as active listening, dialogue, and consensus building. These disciplines are about making space in our hearts, minds, and lives for the experience and understanding that others bring to the table. We let go of our need and/or impulses toward uniformity and see that the diversity among us (even when it seems irreconcilable) is what makes that space sacred. This is not diversity for diversity's sake, but claiming a welcome for everyone. It is about making space for a unity that cannot be achieved ideologically or doctrinally, but only by the unifying power of the Holy Spirit dwelling fully in and among our relationships.

Emptiness is a scary place to be, even if we know it is only a temporary transition to the greater fullness found through the Spirit.

When we rid ourselves of the distractions around us and within us, it is common for the silent cries of our fears and uncertainties to emerge. While it is not at this stage that we are primarily focused on relieving those uncertainties, neither is it right or healthy to deny or reject that they exist. Christians are often made to feel as though our doubts are a failure of faith, almost something sinful.

"Don't be a Doubting Thomas," sung to an upbeat tune, was a children's hymn I would sing almost every week in Sunday school. The message was clear: when the apostle Thomas said that he would not believe that Jesus had risen until he put his hands in His wounds, he proved that he had a lack of faith. Scripture, we were told, proves this out, for when Jesus said, "Have you believed because you have seen me? Blessed are those who have not seen and yet have come to believe" (John 20:29), it was "obvious" that Jesus was clearly rebuking the unfaithful doubt of His follower. Thus, "Don't be a Doubting Thomas" was a refrain heard again and again in one form or another whenever we expressed uncertainty about the complexities, paradoxes, and even contradictions within our faith.

But—my childhood tradition aside—Thomas was not always seen as an illustration for the dangers of doubting. For much of early Church history, the fact that he was able to touch the wounds of Christ was celebrated in word and art as a powerful and beautiful mystical encounter—so much so that it became one of the central stories by which the value of pilgrimages and relics were promoted, citing the significance of physical encounters in faithfulness. While this was not done without acknowledging the affirmation and blessing on those who believed without such physical encounters, it became a source of contention among Protestant Reformers. That movement, predicated significantly on their "by faith alone" theology, developed a deep distrust and eventual rejection of such ideas and practices. Thus, in rejecting the practice of pilgrimage and the use of relics, they chose to read the story of Thomas differently.

In truth, Thomas was being a faithful disciple of Jesus, who warned His disciples that "many will come in my name, saying, 'I am the Messiah!' and they will lead many astray" (Matt. 24:5). Indeed, Jesus affirms those who believe without seeing because such belief takes great faith. But that in no way suggests we should ignore evidence when it is available, as though doing so makes us more faithful. This impulse, combined with an often uncritical biblicism, not only neglects God's command to love him with our minds, but leads us into unnecessary divisiveness and shallow literalism that blinds us to the deeper truth of Scripture. Therefore, during this process of self-emptying, we must be aware of and honest with our uncertainties. While we should never throw around our doubt with rebellious defiance, neither should we view our genuine questions and uncertainties as liabilities. Sometimes allowing ourselves to question deeply held beliefs opens us up to discovering that we were, in fact, in error, offering us the opportunity for more faithful understanding. Other times we discover that our fears are unfounded, returning to our former beliefs without doubt, yet stronger for it.

Again, what is critical to remember in this stage of embracing emptiness is that we do so motivated by love. And, because of this, it is an emptiness that is rooted in hope:

> The spirituality of death that had previously possessed our beings has been "exorcised" and replaced with the animating and life-giving Spirit of Jesus. The cross represents this death, a death that points to a kenostic indifference that creates the space and capacity to love. This is a death that brings about the possibility of resurrection.[24]

In the midst of it all, we didn't know how Beth and Alan's story would end. However, through the redemptive power of God, even the "worst" outcomes are not without real hope. It is a hope in the resurrection of Jesus Christ, which we will share in, and the promise that our emptiness will be filled with the loving and unifying presence of the Holy Spirit. Similarly, St. Patrick, after years of enslavement, finally accepting his lot and giving his fate over to God, would go on to experience new life in ways he could never have imagined possible—a hope we, too, can embrace.

CHAPTER 5

Into Resurrection

So if anyone is in Christ, there is a new creation:
everything old has passed away;
see, everything has become new!
—2 CORINTHIANS 5:17

The dream came one night without warning. In many ways, it was the last thing that Patrick expected. He finally seemed to have found peace within himself, coming to accept his portion in life as a slave among the tribes that captured him. Life was by no stretch easy, but his new and growing faith in God filled him with a hope that went beyond his circumstances. So he dedicated himself fully to the responsibilities he had been given. He would be the best slave he could possibly be.

At first, his newfound loyalty to his masters was met with suspicion. Then, when he explained that he did his duty out of faithfulness to his God and His Son, Jesus, they laughed, mocking him and his weak God. However, because he was going far beyond in his service, they grudgingly accepted his new religious zeal. As long as he kept working and doing his duty, why worry? In their own way, they began to respect Patrick, as far as one respects a slave, that is. He was given greater responsibility in the village and, with it, greater freedom. This was his life, and it was, at least, tolerable.

And so, when the dream came, Patrick was not sure he believed it. Or even wanted to believe it. However, he knew the dream was from God. What had God said to Him in this dream? That his moment of freedom was at hand. God was going to liberate Patrick from slavery and return him to his people. A voice assured him that his moment of liberation had come, that he should make his escape and go to the coast where a ship awaited him.

With such a slim possibility of hope and the threat of death should he be captured, Patrick was hesitant to respond to this promise from God. And yet, he had learned to let go and to trust God, no longer bound to fear and self-preservation. His life was God's, and if God called him to risk what little he had, who was he to disobey?

With that resolute faithfulness in his heart, Patrick slipped away in the night and began to make his way through the wilderness toward the coast. Avoiding villages and roads at all cost, the young slave trusted the leading of God into the unknown. Traveling more than two hundred miles, he finally found the coast. Covering his slave collar as best he could, he made his way into a coastal town in search of a boat. Despite God's promise of freedom, it took everything in Patrick's ability to convince the captain to take him aboard. Then, he watched with an unexpected ache as the land of his captors disappeared behind him as he sailed to freedom.

It was not an easy journey—one interrupted time and again by challenges—but true to God's word, Patrick found himself walking down the dusty road toward Bannaventa, the same road he rode on with his father on the fateful day of his capture. However, while it was the same road, he was not the same person. Gone was the entitled and selfish youth he once was. Patrick returned as the prodigal son transformed by the love and grace of Father God. He walked those last miles toward home considering in his heart the subject of that parable of Jesus, made the more powerful when he looked up to see his own father sprinting toward him to welcome him home. The son who was once lost was found again. He was dead, but was once again alive, in more ways than one.

ARE WE REALLY ALONE BEFORE GOD?

For many of us, the emphasis on what it means to be a Christian has been explicitly individual. We are taught that being part of a church community is essential, but then the focus is placed on our personal responsibility to attend. In many of our churches, even salvation gets framed as an individual transformation, a lone decision between ourselves and Jesus, who becomes our "personal Lord and Savior." Even participating in Communion, while practiced in the context of the congregation, can often be reduced to a silent moment of private piety and personal reflection. In other words, just as Patrick's freedom from captivity found culmination in his restoration among those he loved, so is our liberty a gateway into restored and active relationship with God and others.

Community is the inevitable and essential result of faithfulness, inseparably linked to the work of God in our hearts and in the world. Having humbly exposed and repented of the pretense that kept us in bondage to fear, we are able to divest ourselves of the sinful impulses of selfishness and self-preservation. Choosing to empty our hearts of anything that would compete for our faithfulness to Jesus, we make room for the new life born within us through the work of the Holy Spirit among us. It is not enough that we die with Christ, but we must also share in His resurrection as members of His Body, the Church.

The image of St. Patrick emerging from the wilderness, believed to be dead, yet returning home to his family, alive and well, humbled and transformed, is a familiar image to Christians who know the gospels. We can well imagine Patrick's father declaring, "This son of mine was dead and is alive again; he was lost and is found!" (Lk. 15:24). The resurrection life that Patrick experienced, while it included the transformation of his character, was embodied in the restored relationship he could now enjoy with those he loved and who loved him. So is our resurrection with Christ linked to our relationship with others. The nature of sin is to kill and destroy— it causes disintegration. It breaks down relationships, separating us from God, from creation, and from one another through fear and shame. Thus, the imagery of resurrection being linked to reconciliation with others is critical. Indeed, both the story of the prodigal son and that of Patrick's own return to his family are powerfully fitting images through which to understand the idea of entering into Christ's restorative community.

But for many of us, while valued and affirmed, the idea of community is seen as little more than an important, yet secondary, part of faith. Instead, the focus is on our "individual relationship with God," with the church simply being a place where people of commonly held ideals gather for worship and communion, rather than the mysterious, tangible embodiment of Christ's presence. This is a distortion of the gospel. Our reconciliation with God is critical, but it is inseparable from our reconciliation with each other. In fact, God seems to point to the latter as an essential, even primary means to the former.

Other New Testament texts are important, too. In 2 Corinthians 5:18 we read that Christ has "given us the ministry of reconciliation." Often we interpret that to mean that we're called to evangelize, helping others come into the loving grace and forgiveness of Christ, reconciling with God. Without question, this is one aspect of what God calls us to. However, as we read Scripture, it becomes clear that one of the means by which we are to be reconciled to God (and to help others reconcile to God) is through reconciliation with one another. Too often, Christians put aside reconciliation with others as secondary, focusing instead on their relationship with God, even going so far as to say that until they are "right" with God they can't focus on getting right with others. This may sound appropriately spiritual, but it can also be another form of selfishness and self-preservation, putting our salvation ahead of that of others.

Consider also Ephesians 2:14–18, with respect to reconciliation between Jew and Gentile:

> For he is our peace; in his flesh he has made both groups into one and has broken down the dividing wall, that is, the hostility between us. He has abolished the law with its commandments and ordinances, that he might create in himself one new humanity in place of the two, thus making peace, and might reconcile both groups to God in one body through the cross, thus putting to death that hostility through it. So he came and proclaimed peace to you who were far off and peace to those who were near; for through him both of us have access in one Spirit to the Father.

Notice the order in which this process of reconciliation takes place. First, the boundaries that divide us as people are transformed: "in his flesh he has made both groups into one and has broken down the dividing wall." It is only then, after we break down the barriers between people, that the human-divine relationship is transformed, "that he might create in himself one new humanity in place of the two, thus making peace, and might reconcile both groups to God." Human reconciliation precedes reconciliation between humanity and God.

Taking it further, Jesus affirmed this emphasis clearly in Matthew 5:23, 24:

> So when you are offering your gift at the altar, if you remember that your brother or sister has something against you, leave your gift there before the altar and go; first be reconciled to your brother or sister, and then come and offer your gift.

Again, the pattern is clear. Before you offer your gift to God—a gift for which the purpose is explicitly to reconcile ourselves with God through sacrificial offering—you are to go first to your sister or brother with whom you need to be reconciled. Jesus goes so far as to command us to love our enemies, forgiving others for their sins against us, for "if you do not forgive others, neither will your Father forgive your trespasses" (Matt. 6:15). We cannot separate our love for and reconciliation with one another from our love for and reconciliation with God. As we reconcile with other people—

women and men created in the image of God—we are taking the first steps to reconcile with the very God in whose image we (and they) are created. Therefore, the quality of the relationships we have together as Christians—our community of Christ—reflects the most explicit form of faithfulness in our call to reconciliation.

It was not enough for Patrick to return physically to his family, but like the prodigal son, he was transformed in such a way that his posture toward others had been changed. He was a new man. Part of that process was an unflinching confession of his former nature, which he recounted with brave specificity in his later writings. This tells me that it can be a temptation to acknowledge our sinfulness in abstract generalizations—but whenever possible, the forgiveness we seek should be vulnerably specific.

In AA, steps 8 and 9 provide a clear, if difficult, model for how to approach such a commitment to repentance:

8. Made a list of all persons we had harmed, and became willing to make amends to them all.
9. Made direct amends to such people wherever possible, except when to do so would injure them or others.

Notice how specific the tasks are. A physical list is written citing actual people whom the person negatively impacted in specific ways. In addition to an apology, the person is committed to making restitution, reparation, or restoration whenever possible or appropriate.

I cringe at the thought of this explicit, tangible intentionality regarding my sinfulness. I must face the people I have harmed with my selfish and sinful choices and seek to make things right, to see God's kingdom come in our relationships here and now as they might be in heaven. In other words, the transformation in my heart must bear fruit in my life and in my relationships. *Being* sorry and *saying* sorry might be an important part of that process, but it is not enough. I must do what I can to restore that which I have participated in breaking.

THE WITNESS OF FAILURE

Do we honestly believe that the best witness we can have as Christians before a watching world is to show moral perfection? While that might convince some, our odds of pulling it off seem less than slim. In truth, the most compelling witness to our faith can be a willingness to humbly accept responsibility for our failings and seek to restore relationships at any cost.

For example, when Australian social workers arrived to address the problems in an Aboriginal community in Queensland, a representative from the community, Lilla Watson, stepped forward and beautifully demonstrated this wisdom: "If you have come here to help me, you are wasting your time. But if you have come because your liberation is bound up with mine, then let us work together." Jesus, of course, first understood that such love would be what turns the eyes of the world toward us, authenticating us as His followers: "By this everyone will know that you are my disciples, if you have love for one another" (John 13:35). The work at becoming and being community, then, is at the very heart of the gospel of Jesus Christ, uniting us as His Body for His purpose and for His glory.

The notion of our salvation uniting us as the Church might seem romantic and compelling. It is one of the greatest and most beautiful gifts we will ever receive. Yet, the reason we so rarely see genuine community among Christians is because achieving that reality is far more difficult and demanding than we're often willing to accept. After all, it is a community forged in the painful process of dying to self—not just once, but taking up that cross daily as we faithfully pursue Christ. While difficult, the difficulty is a grace of God. It teaches us that, as His Body, we must see with His eyes, transforming our judgments of others into humble appreciation, which in turn leads to mutual transformation.

In *Life Together*, Dietrich Bonhoeffer reminds us:

Christian community is like the Christian's sanctification. It is a gift of God which we cannot claim. Only God knows the real state of our fellowship, of our sanctification. What may appear weak and trifling to us may be great and glorious to God. Just as the Christian should not be constantly feeling his spiritual pulse, so, too, the Christian community has not been given to us by God for us to be constantly taking its temperature. The more thankfully we daily receive what is given to us, the more surely and steadily will fellowship increase and grow from day to day as God pleases.[25]

We are transformed together into the Body of Christ by grace (not merit), but this identity is more fully realized through the exercise of our free will—choosing again and again to die to self, placing the love of God and others as our first priority. In other words, we realize that it is hard work to become and sustain true community, and recognize that any true community is an unmerited grace.

Community is a grace because of how it serves us in the very process of transformation. When Beth considered the state of her marriage, about how often Alan had repeated his pattern of behavior over and over in the past, she was close to despairing. But she recognized that there was a difference this time, even if only for herself: now they were part of a community that loved them and was committed to open, honest, and unwavering accountability and support. Where in the past their communities attempted to support them, they did so without the commitment of mutual authenticity and brokenness. On those earlier occasions, when some of those friends heard about their struggle, several came forward admitting to having experienced similar encounters with Alan. Instead of lovingly exposing that brokenness in the hope of restoration, they kept quiet, distanced themselves, and "didn't get involved." In the end, while Alan remained responsible for his choices, their choices contributed to the problem persisting and becoming entrenched in their marriage. But this time, in the midst of genuine community, those patterns were immediately (and again, lovingly) exposed and addressed.

I CONFESS

Such community, by nature and necessity, reflects relationships of deep intimacy and vulnerability. This raises the inevitable question: can we trust each other enough to be that vulnerable?

We all have fears and failings that hold us in bondage, but the idea of sharing them with others can be crippling. Yet, the desire to do so seems to be hardwired into our nature as people, despite our sinful impulse resisting it.

Consider the PostSecret phenomenon. PostSecret is a community art project in which people anonymously send in their secrets in artistic form, which are then shared online for anyone to see. They vary in theme, from items as innocuous as the one that reads:

"I steal TP from the gym…. I haven't bought any in 2 years."[26]

To ones revealing emotional woundedness:

"The one race that meant the most to me, you wern't [sic] there to see it. You didn't ask, but I came in first."[27]

To the utterly devastating, yet impossibly hopeful:

"I got pierced after you raped me. Three years later, I have taken it out. I don't need a piece of metal to remind me anymore. I survived."[28]

Since its inception, PostSecret has collected and shared thousands of these anonymous posts, sparking museum exhibits, the publication of books, and international, multilingual spin-offs. So much could be said about this movement, but one thing seems clear: there is a desire in the hearts of so many of us to be free enough to share the secrets we feel must be kept hidden.

I would say that, at its best (while always being mindful of the dangers of idealism), the community of Christ is the relational context where such freedom should be found. And not only should we be able to simply share with honesty, but create a confessional sharing space/place that allows us to prayerfully and lovingly walk with people into forgiveness, wholeness, and into their true, whole selves within the context of community.

That St. Patrick's most widely read work is called *The Confession* is no coincidence. Confession was essential to his development into the saint he became, and like community, it can take many expressions within Christian practice. It includes expressions such as the formal confession between a person and their priest or the practice of general absolution in a wider, congregational context. It also extends far beyond these to include relationships of mutuality and love, where members of a community, freed (and being freed) of pretense, share the whole truth about themselves—the good, the bad, and the ugly—without fear of judgment, nor risk of disinterested "acceptance." Whether it is the confession of sin done to another, seeking out their forgiveness, or the confession of vulnerability that seeks support and accountability, or even the nonculpable confession of victimization that seeks safety and healing, each is rooted in relationships whose trust is possible because of the emptiness they have been graced with.

This kind of confession must be handled with great care and discernment. Confession easily becomes a form of sanctified gossip. Who we choose to confess to requires discernment, not only for our own sakes, but for the love of those to whom we confess. Burdening those less mature in their faith, or whose own experience makes your confession unhealthy for them, can cause more harm than good. Confession will always be risky and costly. It is an act of faith and trust in a God of love whose grace extends past the worst possible outcomes, even and especially death, and offers us new life.

Our church, Little Flowers Community, has wrestled with these dynamics, and we have often turned to Alcoholics Anonymous for inspiration. One of the most beautiful models of a healthy, mutually supportive relationship is the sponsor relationship within AA. While most of us will be passingly familiar with what a sponsor is, we often miss how profound the relationship can be. As an alcoholic starts to make progress in recovery, he or she seeks out someone with whom to share the experience, one-on-one and indefinitely. A member of AA will choose a sponsor not long after beginning to work the steps for themselves, especially as they approach the process of making their "searching and fearless moral inventory" and making amends. The sponsor is someone who, like the person they are sponsoring, is themselves working the steps every day, though perhaps further along in the journey to provide insight and understanding. They do not replace going to meetings and the need for the larger group, but serve as additional support. They are to be trusted to share anything and everything with, in confidence. They are not counsellors or therapists, but they give peer advice when necessary, which is carefully considered by the recipient (though not uncritically accepted). Adapting for our context, we have begun to form these kinds of intentional and supportive relationships in our church community.

What we found to be most critical about sponsors is the mutuality with which the relationship is premised. A sponsor who is twenty years sober is only one drink away from being back at day one, while the person they are sponsoring, sober for only three months, suddenly is in a position to support them. The relationship is not about positional authority but about dynamic mutuality. This is the kind of relationship that we need as we seek to become a confessional people. Sponsors do not replace the roles and functions of pastors and priests, but rather come alongside as an individual support for any time there is a need. The sponsor is not condescendingly helping those beneath her, but is lovingly serving them, paying forward the grace they received from those who supported her. As the sponsor is herself living into restoration, every opportunity to support others strengthens her own resolve to keep the faith.

Therefore, with care, discernment, and practiced disciplines, confession has become an essential part of life in our community: not merely as a means of cleansing ourselves of moral stains, but also rather to free us from the bondage of our fear and shame, allowing us to truly and freely expose our brokenness, find liberty, and love God and others more authentically and sacrificially. This freedom comes significantly through actually getting to know (and be known by) God and others.

The result is loving unity. This is why confession is so closely linked to Communion, the Eucharist, since it is far more about what we are becoming than how we have failed. Fulfilling the paradoxical promise we read in 2 Corinthians 12:10—"for whenever I am weak, then I am strong"—our weaknesses and failures are redeemed, allowing us to genuinely and humbly connect with one another in true community. M. Scott Peck writes:

> Begin to appreciate each others' gifts, and you begin to appreciate your own limitations. Witness others share their brokenness, and you will become able to accept your own inadequacy and imperfection. Be fully aware of human variety, and you will recognize the interdependence of humanity. As a group of people do these things—as they become a community—they become more and more humble, not only as individuals but also as a group—and hence more realistic.[29]

This process invites us into a life where we embrace these disciplines and truth daily, recognizing that we will repeat them again as often as we fail (which will be often). The temptation to do it once and think we are done is seductive. This is why members of AA learn in step 10 that the process of working the steps, of taking personal inventory and making things right, is a process they must repeat over and over again. They do so with the hope that each time they are transformed a little more into the image of God, freed that much more from the bondage to the fear of death. It is less like an endless cycle and more like ascending a mountain, going around and around what seems to be the same path again and again, while every step leads closer to our destination.

The practices and disciplines of building and sustaining community could fill volumes (and has). From mystics to anthropologists, we learn how critical the quality of a community is to the health and well-being of people. Yet, community remains one of the most elusive goals to so many of the Christians and churches in our individualistic Western societies. When we encounter true community, we are not encountering mere healthy relationships of equality and moral uprightness, but we are witnessing, and being invited to participate in, the divine nature of God.

This brings us back to St. Patrick's story, as he returns to the embrace of his family and community. We could easily end our journey there, too, celebrating our freedom from the bondage to the fear of death and restoration to new life. We could celebrate as prodigals come home—once dead, but now alive again—transformed and renewed into the image of Christ, welcomed into His family, community, into His very Body. Yet, also like Patrick's story, the journey does not end there. For as we truly become the Body of Christ together, we then find ourselves caught up in something far bigger than we could imagine: the passionate pursuit of God ensues in His desire to bring every single person into loving, restorative relationship with Him, with others, and with all of creation.

CHAPTER 6

Pentecost

*The Pentecost of the upper room in Jerusalem is
the beginning, a beginning which endures.*

—POPE FRANCIS

P atrick, we cannot lose you again!"

His mother's words stung his heart, but he
knew they were simply an expression of her
love. Surrounded by family and friends, Patrick had called them
together to give them some important news. God had called
him to return to the lands across the seas, where he had been
enslaved, to be his ambassador, a missionary for his kingdom.
At first, his words were met with stunned silence and disbelief,
followed by angry protests and desperate pleading. Then they
all fell silent. His mother's words broke that silence, speaking
for everyone present.

In the years since his return, Patrick's family had celebrated the miracle of his liberation as a gift from God. That he returned transformed in heart, devoted to God in every way, was beyond their expectations. They had affirmed his decision to pursue further religious education and the taking of vows, despite their hope that he would carry on the traditions of the family.

Never could his family and friends have anticipated his return to Ireland. How could they? Not even Patrick had expected a vocation to the place of his servitude. Yet, it had come in a vision too clear to deny. As he later explained,

> I had a vision in my dreams of a man who seemed to come from Ireland: his name was Victoricius and he carried countless letters, one of which he handed over to me. I read aloud where it began: "The Voice of the Irish." And as I began to read these words I seemed to hear the voice of the same men who lived beside the forest of Foclut, which lies near the Western sea where the sun sets. They seemed to shout aloud to me "as if with one and the same voice": "Holy broth of a boy, we beg you, come back and walk once more among us."[30]

Patrick knew instantly upon hearing those words what they meant. God was calling him to return to the land of the Irish to be His witness. God had returned him home, raised him from a kind of death to new life, yet that life belonged to God. He was God's instrument, called to obey regardless of the cost.

"Are you sure this is what God wants?" they asked. "Have you not suffered enough? It is only one dream, after all. Surely God would not call you to give up so much with so little to go by." Patrick smiled with sympathetic understanding, but shook his head.

"No, this is not the only word I have received from God—though had it been, it would be enough, for I know the call of God when I hear it. I also heard God's voice assure me. He said, 'He who gave his own soul for you, He it is who now speaks within your soul.' My calling is clear. I must trust in God, and you must entrust me into His hands once again."

So it was, with the reluctant blessing of his family, that Patrick found himself once again in a boat leaving the shores of his youth, leaving family and friends and home behind, to go into the unknown. But things were different this time. No longer bound in body and spirit, He stood free in every way through the liberty that Christ graced him with. No longer alone, he went with brothers equally devoted to this mission, even at the cost of their lives. They went with God's presence felt deeply among them, the Holy Spirit binding them together and empowering them to be ministers of reconciliation and love among the lost.

TRANSFORMATION AFTER TRAGEDY

Recently, Delia, a member of our community, told me a story about a tragic and remarkable encounter she had many years ago. One day, she and her husband, along with their three young sons, were traveling as passengers in her in-law's van. Dozing quietly in the back of the vehicle with the kids, they were suddenly startled awake by cries of alarm from her father-in-law, followed by a cracking thud, with the van braking and swerving to the side, coming to a rough and angled halt. Both Delia and her husband are blind, so they called out in concern, asking what happened.

As they were driving down the road, a young boy—about the age of her own sons—was riding his bike along the right shoulder. Without warning or even so much as a glance over his shoulder to check for cars, the boy had swerved across the road toward the driveway on the opposite side of the highway. Despite hitting the brakes and swerving sharply away, the van slammed into the boy, whose body bounced off the windshield before being thrown brutally across the pavement. It was clear that the boy was seriously injured, as the van came to a stop across the very driveway the boy had been turning into.

A passing driver who had witnessed the event quickly pulled over, assuring Delia's father-in-law that they had seen everything and would testify that there was nothing he could have done to prevent the accident. They were informed that 911 had been called and that an ambulance was en route. It turned out that the house belonging to the driveway was home to family members of the young boy, aunt and uncle and cousins. Apparently, he often rode along the highway to visit his relatives. With traffic rare on this stretch, he almost never needed to watch for vehicles. Delia and her family were crushed, their grief turned to guilt as they sat waiting among the family whose lives they had just devastated.

Soon, a grief-stricken woman arrived, who they soon learned was something of an adoptive mother to the boy, having taken him in as her own because of family circumstances, loving him as though she had given birth to him herself. Collapsing alongside the road, she watched in tears as someone tirelessly performed CPR on the broken body as they all waited for an ambulance to arrive. His injuries were visibly serious, and the distance to the nearest hospital made quick medical intervention impossible. Even if the boy had been wearing a helmet, which he hadn't been, it seemed unlikely that he would have survived. All Delia and her family could do was wait and watch in stunned grief and regret, unable even to move the van until police arrived to thoroughly examine the scene. So they stood there, surrounded by the friends and family of the boy, until the ambulance finally arrived.

Unexpectedly, a man approached them. Introducing himself as a minister, they learned that the family, as well as their wider community, were Holdeman, a small Mennonite sect named after one of their original leaders, John Holdeman. Like their global brethren, this community chose to share lives of simplicity and deep devotion to the teachings of Jesus. Smiling, the minister asked Delia's boys if they were hungry (which they were, since lunch had come and gone), informing them that the homeowners—the aunt and uncle and cousins of the young boy—had invited them into their home to share a meal. Stunned, they gratefully accepted the unexpected kindness. And as they ate, the grieving family made it clear that they fully understood that no one had done anything wrong; it was just a tragedy for which they held no ill will.

Time slowly passed, with the police continuing to investigate, keeping their van off limits for hours. The minister, having left earlier, returned with a van of his own, inviting Delia and her family to a "change of scenery," a kindness they gratefully accepted. As they met him outside the house, he sadly informed them that the young boy had succumbed to his injuries and died before arriving at the hospital. Leaving the family to grieve in peace, the minister drove Delia's family to a local restaurant, where they waited over coffee and snacks. Hearing about the events, the sympathetic restaurant owners refused to let them pay for anything, telling them that it was all on the house. Everyone in the community, while deeply broken by the sudden and senseless death of the young boy, refused to let anger or bitterness take root. Instead, they showed an empathy and compassion toward those who so desperately needed it. Even months later, the community made the effort to assure Delia's father-in-law that they held nothing against him. Delia will never forget that beautiful gift of grace extended to them.

What amazing grace exists that allows a people to face this kind of tragedy and respond in such a way? It would have been enough for them to simply withhold judgment or blame. That would have been a witness of their forgiveness. Yet, the Holdeman community knew that they had to go beyond that, recognizing that the brokenness of the events touched everyone involved, not just their own. Instead of anger, they were able to feel compassion for the suffering the driver and the passengers were feeling. They responded with that radical grace.

This is the fruit of transformation that only God can produce in us. This is the kind of people we are becoming as we pursue wholeness and freedom in Christ. Even in the midst of great suffering and loss, the witness (*martos* in Greek) of Christ can be made manifest in how we live. Sometimes, I think, it is even and especially in these situations that it is most powerfully seen and heard.

As we consider St. Patrick's story, if we were able to erase from our memories the fact that he would later return to the land of his captors to bear witness to Christ, his liberation from slavery and return to his family would have been the quintessential happy ending. After all, not only was he freed from the literal chains of slavery, but he had been freed from the bondage of sin as well. Transformed into the kind of godly man both his father and grandfather always hoped he would become—even beyond their expectations—he'd dedicated himself to God upon his return, becoming a cleric. He had suffered more in those years as a slave than most will experience in a lifetime, yet he refused to let despair or hatred win. It is hard not to argue that his freedom was well deserved. A great way to finish a story, a perfect "happily ever after."

However, Patrick did not see things that way. He knew that his life—his resurrection to *new* life—was a gift. With lessons learned through years in slavery, he began to empty himself of selfishness, pride, and fear, dedicating himself to God in prayer. Patrick understood what was needed to continue producing humility, repentance, and above all, obedience. He had been transformed into the image of Christ and therefore could do nothing else but be about the work of Christ in the world.

Patrick understood that his freedom from bondage was not an end, but that his liberty allowed him to more clearly discern the call of God in his life. Like the wisdom of AA's eleventh step, he seemed to understand that "through prayer and meditation" he could "improve [his] conscious contact with God," "praying only for knowledge of His will for [him] and the power to carry that out." In other words, the self-emptying of *kenosis* produced in him a space that was filled with the Spirit of God. This not only raised him to new life, but gave him clarity to discern and obey the will of God for his life from that point forward, no matter the cost. For him, following Jesus meant returning to the home and hearth of his enemies, enemies he was called by Jesus to love. If he was going to love his enemies, he would have to seek them out, entering again into their world, regardless of the risk it presented to him. In so doing, he becomes an example to us. As Bonhoeffer reminds us:

> The Christian cannot simply take for granted the privilege
> of living among other Christians. Jesus Christ lived in the
> midst of his enemies. In the end all his disciples abandoned
> him. On the cross he was all alone, surrounded by criminals

and the jeering crowds. He had come for the express purpose of bringing peace to the enemies of God. So Christians, too, belong not in the seclusion of a cloistered life but in the midst of enemies. There they find their mission, their work.[31]

This characteristic selflessness is not unique to St. Patrick. The lives of the saints demonstrate this willingness again and again. In my own tradition as an Anabaptist, we have many such stories as well. One that stands out particularly to me is the story of Dirk Willems.

Dirk Willems was a Dutch Anabaptist, part of what is often referred to as the Radical Reformation, in the sixteenth century. His commitment to his newfound faith led to his arrest and eventual condemnation by the Roman Catholic Church.[32] Locked in his cell, Willems knew that death was the only verdict he would receive, and so he tried to devise a means of escape. While he was more than willing to die for his faith, he wouldn't do so unless absolutely necessary. So with great ingenuity, he made a rope out of knotted rags and was able to escape out of the tower window. Shimmying down to the ground, his freedom was almost in grasp, and he raced to escape before they discovered him missing.

However, one of the guards spotted Willems and went in immediate pursuit. As he ran, Willems came to a pond, newly covered in a thin layer of ice. Knowing that to go around the pond would likely allow the guard the time he needed to catch up with him, Willems decided to risk it and ran as quickly (and gingerly) as possible across thin ice. By some miracle, the groaning ice held, and he made it safely to the other side.

He was free! Yet, just as he was renewing his quick retreat, he heard a cry from behind him. Turning, he saw that the guard who had been pursuing him, thinking the route across the pond safe, had followed Willems out onto the ice. However, the ice could take no more weight and had collapsed under the man. The panicking guard, who could not swim, was about to drown in the icy waters.

In that moment, Willems responded according to the faith he lived and proclaimed. He knew that he was called by Jesus to love his enemy—and to love his enemy in this moment could mean only one thing: save the drowning man. So, risking his own life once again on the ice and giving up the nearly guaranteed freedom he could have had if he had just kept running, Willems shimmied out onto the ice and pulled the stunned and grateful guard to safety. The guard, moved by this act of selfless love, urged Willems to again run and escape, but by that point it was too late. Other authorities had arrived, placing the escaped "heretic" back into custody and back to his cell. On May 16, 1569, Dirk Willems was burned at the stake. Those were awful times.

St. Patrick, like Dirk Willems, found liberty from the fear of death. With death no longer a threat, he could embrace fully the proactive, selfless love of Christ for his enemies. With new eyes he looked on those who had taken everything from him—those whom most of us, if we found ourselves in his shoes, would fear, if not hate outright—and saw in them the divine image, the hope of the same transformation that he had experienced. There is almost a tone of thankfulness in Patrick's writings, as though he was grateful to his captors for giving him the opportunity to be so transformed, eager to repay such a gift with his loving and lifelong service. Surely this is the fruit born of following Christ to the cross and sharing in His resurrection life. This is something of a Pentecost moment.

TAKING THE SPIRIT SERIOUSLY

Pentecost is when we remember and celebrate the Holy Spirit's descent upon the Apostles following the ascension of the resurrected Christ. Acts 2:1–13 tells us this strange and wonderful story:

> When the day of Pentecost had come, they were all together in one place. And suddenly from heaven there came a sound like the rush of a violent wind, and it filled the entire house where they were sitting. Divided tongues, as of fire, appeared among them, and a tongue rested on each of them. All of them were filled with the Holy Spirit and began to speak in other languages, as the Spirit gave them ability.
>
> Now there were devout Jews from every nation under heaven living in Jerusalem. And at this sound the crowd gathered and was bewildered, because each one heard them speaking in the native language of each. Amazed and astonished, they asked, "Are not all these who are speaking Galileans? And how is it that we hear, each of us, in our own native language? Parthians, Medes, Elamites, and residents of Mesopotamia, Judea and Cappadocia, Pontus and Asia, Phrygia and Pamphylia, Egypt and the

parts of Libya belonging to Cyrene, and visitors from Rome, both Jews and proselytes, Cretans and Arabs—in our own languages we hear them speaking about God's deeds of power." All were amazed and perplexed, saying to one another, "What does this mean?" But others sneered and said, "They are filled with new wine."

In other words, the story of Christ among us in the flesh did not simply end with his resurrection. Instead, Jesus ascended to the Father and, just as the Father sent Him to us, so too did He send the Holy Spirit. Through that gift, a moment that was characterized by uncertainty—where the disciples must surely have been conflicted, torn between the joy of the resurrected and ascended Messiah and the ambiguity of what that now meant for them—is transformed into a powerful display of love and embrace. Just as the chaos of the cross exposed our fear of differences, at Pentecost, by the power of the Holy Spirit, the boundaries of difference (most explicitly those of language and culture, in this case) are transcended.

The listeners were not miraculously able to understand the language of those proclaiming the Good News, but proclaimers miraculously did so in the languages of those listening. In other words, the boundaries that divided them were transcended, yet the uniqueness of each people hearing those words was maintained and celebrated. God did not simply bring the outsiders "inside" by allowing them to understand the language of the insiders, but (as with the Incarnation itself) reached outside the boundaries and spoke to each person in their own tongue.

This is significant, but given the nature of the sacred language of the Jews (Hebrew), it is an even more powerful example of Christ's embrace of the other. Hebrew was the language reserved for the reading of the Torah, for prayer, and for most religious practices. Hebrew was core to what distinguished the Jews as God's chosen people. Therefore, for the Holy Spirit to spark the proclamation of the Good News in the many tongues of the people there—rather than to do so as most would expect, in Hebrew—was a way to further close the gap between God and humanity, between us and the other. The point is this: Pentecost united and empowered God's people to love across boundaries that once divided, placing our own experience, expectations, and rights secondary to those who we are called to love and minister to.

So as St. Patrick embarked on his vocation of love among his enemies, this was his Pentecost moment, that place in his life where the Holy Spirit drew him into the person of Christ, where he saw what Jesus saw, sharing a single heartbeat of love for God and others, even (and perhaps, especially) for his enemies. It was by the power and leading of the Spirit that Patrick could boldly go into the wilds of his former captivity as an agent of grace, mercy, and love.

All of this was only possible on the far side of the cross and the emptiness of the tomb. It was only after he had relinquished his rights to anger, vengeance, or even his entitlement to basic security, that he could be transformed. And he was transformed in such a way that he no longer saw the Irish as his enemies, but rather as his future brothers and sisters in Christ and fellow members in the Church. He believed by faith that as he lovingly lived and proclaim the hope of salvation among the Irish, like on the day of Pentecost, they would hear and understand in ways that transcended barriers and expectations.

Patrick and his missionaries went on to model a respect and engagement of local culture and custom that was unheard of in Christendom at the time, reaching the people in ways that went to their hearts. This might not seem like a necessary statement except that the word *mission* sadly bears the burden of a history of Christian colonialism, dominionism, and racial supremacy that has left it seemingly irreparable in its damaged state. Thankfully, we love and serve a God who is in the business of impossible redemptions. However, in order for us to rediscover and embrace true mission, we must also identify the abuses done in its name (both past and present), repent of those destructive patterns, and begin to live a better alternative. The future of our witness before a watching world depends on it. In fact, such repentance is perhaps our greatest witness.[33]

When we enter into the body of Christ, we receive the universal vocation to be about the work of Jesus in the world. After all, we are His Body, not merely our own.

This is why I have come to love the word *missional*. Rather than a noun (like its root *mission*), missional is an adjective—it becomes a description, rather than the thing itself. When we embrace a *missional* life, we begin to expect that every aspect of who we are and what we do will be infused with Jesus's mission of love. This means that we do not simply *do* a mission, go on a mission, or support mission work, but we *are* a missional people.

This emphasis is directed primarily at the here and now, as Christ-embodying communities of active love in the midst of the world. All of creation is caught up in the restorative work. The mission of God's people is not simply directed at saving people's souls from a bad life-after-death into a good life-after-death, but it addresses and hopefully touches the injustice and violence around us—poverty, racism, sexism, economic exploitation, war, environmental destruction—where salvation, justice, and peace can merge. The holistic mission of St. Patrick, which cared as much for the health, economics, and social fabric of the Irish as for their place in eternity, modeled this restorative theme.

MISSIONAL IS WHO WE ARE

This is not mere activism—or, *it had better not be*—but the natural outpouring of the work God has done in us in liberating us from our pretense, from the bondage to the fear of death. How we live missionally is characterized by the nature of the redemption we have experienced. In other words, just as we have broken free of the fear and boundaries that divide us, now we are a people whose love for each other, for others, and for God is so evident that it stands as an attractive alternative to what is easily seen in the world.

Notice the connection between this experience and what is said in the twelfth and final step in AA's twelve-step program:

> Having had a spiritual awakening as the result of these steps,
> we tried to carry this message to alcoholics, and to practice
> these principles in all our affairs.[34]

This step begins with an acknowledgment of our need to embrace spiritual transformation, while urging us to respond to this gift by going out to those in need of the same. Then, in case we might be foolish enough to think that we have somehow completed our own transformation once and for all, it reminds us that we must continue to be about the work of these steps always, in every aspect of our lives. Rooted in a humility and dependency upon God that everyone can acknowledge, the right posture and motivation for lovingly serving others is clearly established.

This is why we find it important to live close to each other at Little Flowers Community. Most of our members either live with others in co-housing or close to one another in the West End neighborhood where we worship. Such proximity provides practical opportunities to share life together, where we regularly share meals, help each other in times of need (from home repairs to mourning loss), celebrate joy-filled moments, and pursue relationship with God alongside each other and through our relationship with one another. In reflecting these values, we often reiterate the vows of the sisters of Rueilly, a Protestant monastic order in France:

> Receive this cross. It is a sign that you belong to God at the
> heart of our community. From now on, this community is
> yours. And you are responsible, with us, for its fidelity.[35]

For us, to "belong to God at the heart of our community" means two things. First, and perhaps more obviously, it means we are the beloved of the Father, accepted and embraced as His children in the context of our community. However, there is a second meaning that is less common, but which has become very important to us. It also means that we are no longer our own, but that we belong to God, who is our Lord. We belong to God not only as individuals, but at the heart of our community. The relationships and realities of the people in our community become our priority, a realignment of priorities that transcend the rights and expectations of the world. This is a significant, yet beautiful, commitment required of us as followers of Jesus. Surely it is a similar relational commitment that allowed St. Patrick to leave his family and pursue God's mission of love among the Irish.

As we share life of mutual belonging in proximity with each other, we intentionally do so while participating in the fabric of our neighborhood, as we try to live out Christ's love in ways that are most meaningful in our particular context. We find ourselves shopping together, playing together, working together, and living together. It is through active relationship and service to (and with) our neighbors that our witness becomes embodied and more meaningful. I think this lends our community a humble authority and a certain measure of credibility in our neighborhood.

This way of living is highly countercultural, not only in the wider context of society, but to the status-quo subculture of much of Christianity today. Embracing these values and practices of missional community can exact a high cost. They cannot simply be added to our existing lives as mere ideology or as a set of abstract values; we have to embody them. As we face the challenges to embracing this way of life, we will find ourselves again at the start of the process. We will once again find ourselves needing to expose the nakedness of our selfishness, perhaps unwillingness to let go of our pretense and privilege. In this way, this process is a cycle that will repeat itself through our lives, as individuals and as communities, drawing us closer to the heart of God each time.

And it doesn't end there. Far more than just being countercultural, this way of life defies our basic common sense and survival instincts. After all, we have come through the transforming work of Christ, finding ourselves living in freedom from the fear of death. But it is here that we are able to embrace our "martyrological" identity. Imagine what we might do for the kingdom of God if we genuinely didn't fear death. Imagine what we might dare to try if we did not care about social rejection. Imagine what we could create if we did not limit ourselves and our imaginations by the seeming impossibilities of circumstances, but embraced the command to "seek first the kingdom of God and His righteousness." It is out of this kind of missional imagination that the kingdom breaks forth impossibly into the world, and God's loving reign is occasionally seen.

It is in the face of this radical revisioning of ourselves as the community of Christ that our relationship to "the least of these" is formed. They don't represent a threat to our lives, both physically (in their demands on our resources, in the loss of safety) and existentially (in how they expose our pretense, our privilege), but they actually can be seen as Christ Himself. Not in some romantic, shallow way in which we take in the homeless beggar only to have him later throw off his rags to reveal himself as Jesus, rewarding us for our righteousness. No, we encounter Christ in them because the process we have gone through has demonstrated to us that in the *other*—in those most different from us—our own inadequacy is exposed, offering us the opportunity to embrace the gift of the transforming cross.

In the chaos of overcoming and celebrating differences, we become more like the God in whose Trinitarian nature we have been created. The very *otherness* of the least of these brings with it something unique about the divine nature that we would never have encountered otherwise. It is exactly that which costs us (or threatens us) in relating to the least of these that is so very essential. We no longer see them for the circumstances which make them *other*, but as fellow people created in the image of God. We see Christ in them. The response to such a vision changes our posture entirely. Where once we sought to *be Christ* to the least of these, we now *see Christ* in them.

How else could Patrick choose to return to a people who brutalized him for years? This is one of the secrets of his baffling transformation.

Consider the significance of this shift: if you encountered a homeless man and decided to act like Jesus toward Him, what might that look like? Perhaps you would feed him, clothe him, affirm his dignity, and tell him that he is loved by God. Without question this is beautiful and important. However, consider it from the other side: if you encountered a homeless man and decided to treat him in the same way you would treat Christ, what might *that* look like? How might your posture be different? The contrast becomes very clear. Despite the value of the former, with such an approach we are still more or less coming to the man with a posture of superiority, aren't we? The *haves* coming to help the *have-nots*, so to speak. We are his savior.

When truly treating him like he is Jesus, everything would be reversed. Suddenly, our approach to the man is not as someone who is in need of what we have to offer, but as humble servants called to treat him with a dignity and respect. This perspective recognizes that this person has as much to offer us as we do him, maybe even more. It is in this way that we need the poor more than they need us. Or, more honestly, as we humbly relate to the poor, our own poverty is exposed. Either way, in treating the homeless as Jesus, the transformation is mutual, not one-sided. It is a beautiful twist, as we attempt to treat the other as though we are serving Christ. When we *see Jesus* in the least and act accordingly, it is only then that we ourselves begin to *be like Jesus* in appropriate ways, becoming servants of all.

This doesn't just happen. It requires an intentionality that moves us from where we are to where they are, in the same way that God became man and dwelt among us—and in the same way that St. Patrick went to live among the Irish. And as with Patrick, such a commitment requires willing and costly obedience.

For our Little Flowers Community it has meant choosing to live in a neighborhood that had been abandoned by other Christians (and people of privilege in general). There we found "the least of these": the poor, prostitutes, and a vast immigrant community. Here again is the importance of intentional proximity. It sometimes means moving where you live in obedience to God (as Patrick did). And it surely also always means reorienting our lives in such a way that we encounter the other regularly and naturally. We have a saying in our community that reminds us of this: when God said to his people in Deuteronomy 15:4 that "there should be no poor among you" (NIV), He wasn't suggesting segregation.

THE BOON OF BROKENNESS

There were few people who were more *other* to St. Patrick than the people who had held him like an animal in captivity. Yet, he chose to relocate his life among them, at total risk and cost to himself in doing so. That is in no small way why he went on to be one of the most celebrated Christians in history. It might be easy for us, reading the hagiographies of his life, to assume that St. Patrick had arrived at a state of spiritual maturity so great that we could never expect (or be expected) to aspire to such an example. However, we know that he was also a man like every other, faced daily with fear and temptation. And a reading of his life and his own words reveals that he was not without fault, but had to confront his own pretense and bondage to fear over and over again.

Having experienced such a transformation, Patrick had the faith to face his challenges and overcome them more and more. When he failed, he found freedom in repentance, and so was able to give his life in loving service to others, wholly and completely. His story did not end at his choice to return to the land of his slave masters; in many respects, that's where his story really begins. In the same way, when we choose together to enter into the fullness of our shared and Spirit-empowered vocation to love God and others, our lives truly begin. It is here that we encounter the fullness of life promised to us by Jesus Christ.

Consider again the twelfth and final step in AA's twelve-step program:

> Having had a spiritual awakening as the result of these steps,
> we tried to carry this message to alcoholics, and to practice
> these principles in all our affairs.

What this means is that, having done the grueling, hard job of working the steps, again and again, I am allowing God to transform me into something new, something different than when I first began the process.

In the same way, the process of vulnerable faith has led us on a journey of transformation that is accomplished by the mystery of God's grace and the power of the Holy Spirit as we faithfully and obediently do our part together. Such a transformation gives authority and credibility to the task of carrying this hope to others.

Whether you are in a process of Christian formation or in the midst of AA's twelve steps, we are all tempted to rush past each step in the process of transformation and in our eagerness and zeal. This is a good impulse that can have a positive impact on others. The catharsis we feel early on, such as when we expose our pretense and bring into the light the shame and fear that keep us bound, can feel like a transformation unto itself. And in small ways, it is. However, it can produce in us a confidence premature to our place on the journey. It can become an escape mechanism for the hard work that we must do together in facing our chaos, letting go and embracing the *kenotic* emptiness, to really and truly bring us to new life. In other words, we must walk the walk in order to talk the talk.

There is a mystical transformation that takes place beyond our comprehension, but it is never separate from the devotion and discipline required by costly faithfulness. Why else would Jesus call us to take up our cross daily and follow Him? Why else would He leave for us the stunning and overwhelming gift of the gospels? Jesus calls us to tangible, lifelong changes to how we perceive and respond to life, both the good and the bad. This is the recognition of conversion, body and soul; mind, will, and emotions.

This doesn't mean that we have to achieve some level of perfection before we can reach out to others with the love of Christ—that would set an impossible standard. Further, most people would see through this as falsehood and hypocrisy, rejecting us and our message out of hand. Instead, being free to name and acknowledge our individual and communal (and even religious) failings, repenting where necessary, demonstrates the reality of the ongoing work of God in our lives. It means that we can see ourselves in our brokenness, but people can also glimpse in us the hope and love possible in the midst of that same brokenness. A vulnerable faith makes this possible.

In fact, vulnerable faith produces in us a grace and patience for the same failings in others that we have admitted in ourselves. We are no longer motivated to judge others to bolster our own sense of righteousness or protect our own moral purity, but are drawn to those who need grace and hope. I have to keep reminding myself that openness and vulnerability are what I am called to. "After all," I often think to myself, "too many people look up to me in my church for me to admit this failure. Better that I should privately repent before God." Or, in the guise of compassion, I think, "To confess this would hurt someone. Why should I put my forgiveness ahead of their well-being? I'll just bring it to God." But I've learned that this kind of thinking leaves me caught in the bondage that pretense produces, and it robs others of the hope that could come from my honesty and brokenness.

This was once illustrated to our community in a way we could never have anticipated. About five years ago I watched my friend Andrew, a gifted young artist with untreated mental illness, jump to his death from a building down the street from my house. Andrew was an early member of our church. A new Christian, brought to faith by his sister, he was beginning to find new life and hope amid the brokenness of his life. Sadly, we were not able to get him the help he needed in time. And so, in a cloud of confusion and fear, he took the only escape he felt was available to him. As he fell to his death that day, our community fell into a chaos of grief and uncertainty.

Confronted by this stunning blow, we slowly began to pick up the pieces and support one another in our grief. And in the midst of that recovery, we began to ask hard questions: What might have helped Andrew get the help he needed? Did we do something wrong? How do we, now, respond to the complexities and difficulties of loving and supporting our families, friends, and neighbors who live with mental illness? What can we do differently in the future?

As we considered these questions, many things began to emerge. We started to educate ourselves about mental health. We developed a stronger culture of honesty where people would be free to share their struggles and ask for help. More and more of us began to open our homes to those in need. And we recognized that one of the most stabilizing things that could be extended to people like Andrew was safe housing and supportive friends—similar to what he had started to receive, before his death, when he moved to live with his sister, who cared for and supported him so well. Andrew needed more of that kind of love.

This last point stuck with us. Our existing commitment to intentional co-housing wasn't somehow enough. So we began dreaming of extending our capacity to welcome people like Andrew, providing housing that was both affordable and dignified (a rare thing in our inner-city community), while nurturing strong social supports and a sense of community. Over the next several years, with the support of partners and donors, we were able to purchase and renovate a small apartment building that would serve just such a purpose. In the years where the building was slowly being renovated, even the rumors about the project drew people into our community, many becoming part of our church, some even moving into our homes. At the time of this writing, the building is poised to open to tenants any day now. We have named it Chiara House—for who better to symbolize the radical welcome of the other than St. Clare of Assisi?—and have dedicated the building to Andrew's memory. This is an important piece of what it has meant for our community to embrace our missional identity.

But what it looks like to be missional will vary as widely as the diversity of individuals and communities. Your expressions will look different. You will respond to needs that we have probably not seen and can't even imagine.

What St. Patrick brought to Ireland those centuries ago will not work in my Canadian inner-city neighborhood. It won't work today. What remains the same, however, is that the new life born into a people committed to be about the work of God in the world will bear fruit that surpasses expectations—if not in scale and reach, then in the depth of love upon which even the simplest acts of service can be built. We can take steps of faith together, living into the freedom over fear and selfish desires, in order to see God's kingdom come.

CHAPTER 7

Kingdom Come

Your kingdom come. Your will be done,
on earth as it is in heaven.

—*JESUS*

S t. Patrick scanned the gathering crowd with great interest as he awaited the arrival of his host. Surrounded by men of influence and wealth among their people, he found it disconcerting how they deferred to him as an honored guest. As countless servants continually approached him to see to any needs he might have, Patrick pulled unconsciously at his collar where his band of slavery, long since removed, still twanged with phantom discomfort. It was a strange moment to be in that place, considering all that led up to that day.

His thoughts were interrupted by the arrival of his host, none other than King Aengus. Having heard stories about these Christians, the king had become impressed with the nature of this new religion, both in its teaching as well as in the impact it seemed to have among his people. Patrick had helped establish several monastic communities that, in addition to their devotion to Christ, also devoted themselves to the life of the communities they became a part of. Each of these communities experienced sudden growth, with local trade thriving. With the increase in commerce, the locals were able to establish schools, as well as invest in art and culture. In short, under this new Christian faith, the people of Ireland seemed to experience new life on every level. So, learning what he could about these Christians, King Aengus had become convinced that he, too, probably needed to be baptized. So Patrick had been summoned.

This former slave, once barely worthy to care for the pigs of his masters, now stood among their noblemen as an honored man of God, leading the ceremony that would welcome their king into the fold of the Church. Leaning heavily on his crozier, Patrick led the king through the prayers and rituals of his baptism. From the intense expression on the king's face, Patrick assumed him to be deeply moved by this act of devotion he was entering into—and so he continued his prayers.

However, upon finishing the lengthy ceremony, Patrick gasped to see a small pool of blood gathering near his feet. It was only then that he realized that he had accidentally stuck the spiked end of his staff into King Aegnus's foot, piercing it deeply. Startled, Patrick quickly pulled the spike out and encouraged the king's servants to staunch the flow of blood. After a few moments, when Patrick asked King Aengus why he had said nothing, the nobleman shrugged and replied gravely: "I simply assumed it to be a part of the ceremony, and did not consider any suffering that might be required to endure to be of any consequence in order to be welcomed into God's kingdom."

Patrick laughed in spite of himself, leading the limping monarch away. As they walked away, without delay the priest began to tell the king more about the King of Kings he had just chosen to serve and follow. We might laugh, too, and the accuracy of this tale has been questioned by many scholars. However, like every great story in the lives of the saints, I suspect that there is at least a kernel of truth in it.

WHAT'S POSSIBLE

The seeds of transformation were planted among the people under Aengus's command—the same transformation that had led Patrick from the entitled sinfulness of his youth to his devotion to loving service to God and others. Those seeds would go on to transform not only the clans and peoples of Ireland, but the broader Roman Empire of which Ireland was a part and, by extension, Western Christianity itself.

The story of St. Patrick demonstrates how the obedience of one person can make an incredible impact on the course of world history. We are not each of us called to change history, but we are each supposed to be faithful wherever we are called to be. We hold that possibility in our hearts, never underestimating the power of our obedience (or the potential consequences of our unfaithfulness). Patrick is an example of how God can take one person and bring His kingdom into the impossible places in our world, as long as we are willing to live into the work He has for us. While it is hard to keep the big picture in mind as we seek to be faithful in our small corner of the planet and history, it is important to understand the nature of the larger vision our lives are investing in. What does that look like as we live it out together in the world?

Like many Christians I know, I was mostly taught that living into the mission of God meant telling people that Jesus would forgive their sins if they repented, securing for themselves a place in heaven after death, and avoiding the eternal suffering of the flames of hell. And while we can certainly find threads throughout Scripture to explain these emphases, there came a point in my faith journey where I began to see that such a description poorly reflected the hopeful vision that Jesus embodied and proclaimed. While He was certainly concerned with "eternal things," including that which follows death, Jesus seemed far more concerned with the here and now. In fact, as I began to read Scripture more and more, I realized that this emphasis on present reality ran from Genesis through Revelation. Walter Brueggemann identifies this constant and disruptive thread as *shalom*[36]:

> Shalom is the end of coercion. Shalom is the end of fragmentation. Shalom is the freedom to rejoice. Shalom is the courage to live an integrated life in a community of coherence. These are not simply neat values to be added on. They are a massive protest against the central values by which our world operates.[37]

Shalom is what love looks like in the flesh. The embodiment of love in the context of a broken creation, shalom is a hint at what was, what should be, and what will one day be again. Where sin disintegrates and isolates, shalom brings together and restores. Where fear and shame throw up walls and put on masks, shalom breaks down barriers and frees us from the pretense of our false selves. Jesus, the truth incarnate, is the very embodiment of this shalom:

> Jesus, properly understood as shalom, coming into the world from the shalom community of the Trinity, is the intention of God's once-and-for-all mission. That is, the mission of birthing and restoring shalom to the world is in Christ, by Christ, and for the honor of Christ.[38]

And because we are transformed together into the Body of Christ, empowered and united by His Spirit to be about the things He loved, this is the mission in the world we are to participate with Christ in completing. When this happens, the kingdom of God breaks through the brokenness of our world with the promise of salvation and reconciliation.

Shalom is clearly represented throughout the Scriptural narrative—more than talk of the afterlife ever is. It is present in the untouched garden, where the four fundamental relationships God created function in perfect harmony. It is present in every attempt (all the flawed and failed attempts included) of God's people seeking to restore that redemptive order. It is at the heart of every word and deed of Christ. And, it is at the heart of Eucharist.

Yet, for too many Christians, the word and the concept of shalom has never even been introduced or adequately explained. Even in my own experience as a young Christian, while I know it was not willfully withheld, it was as foreign to my Christian leaders as it was to me. But now, I know from personal experience—and have dedicated my life and work to shalom—that shalom is the natural and inevitable product of the redemptive grace of God in my life.

Even the concepts of salvation we find in Scripture, which I had been taught were entirely about being saved from hell as the consequence of my sin, are overwhelmingly infused with this all-encompassing emphasis. One of the reasons we miss this is that it is most often translated in Scripture as the word *peace*. And while this works on many levels, our narrow understanding of peace undermines the richer meanings behind the word *shalom*. *Shalom* is a Hebrew word that means far more than the absence or abating of violence. Central to its meaning is the concept of wholeness—a wholeness that extends to all of creation, but also, and importantly, includes the individual as well:

> It meant well-being, or health, or salvation in its fullest sense, material as well as spiritual. It described the situation of well-being which resulted from authentically whole (healed) relationships among people, as well as between persons and God. According to the Old Testament prophets, shalom reigned in Israel when there was social justice, when the cause of the poor and the weak was vindicated, when there was equal opportunity for all, in short, when the people enjoyed salvation according to the intention of God expressed in his covenant.[39]

So centrally does shalom figure into the Jewish worldview that, to this day, Jewish people the world over greet and part with the words "*shalom aleichem*," which means "shalom unto you." Shalom is what they—it is what I—hope will shape every one of my relationships. Shalom is understood to be extended to family, to social circles, to our economic systems and practices, to regional and national governance and beyond. It is a vision that encompasses all of creation.

Shalom cuts to the heart of our faith, undergirding all of it. In the Old Testament, in the many places where shalom is mentioned, with only a few exceptions it is used to point toward liberation from political, social, and/or economic oppression and hardship—most explicitly in the story of God's people's bondage in slavery to the Egyptians. The second most common usage of shalom refers to social relationships, where the idea of peace is most explicitly linked to it. This describes a justice that is about more than moral upright-ness or the punishing of wrongdoers, but is beautifully about right relationships between people. This is why the Jewish prophets are seen as the voice of God's justice, why they again and again speak out against the exploitation of the weak, most often referenced as the most vulnerable among them: the widows and orphans.

Examples of shalom in reference to personal morality or ethics are, by comparison, few. The quantity of emphasis relative to the other meanings should demonstrate where God calls us to place our attention. Sadly, in our individualistic age, we have reversed this logic and placed personal piety and moral uprightness at the heart of our responsibility as Christians, minimizing (and sometimes outright rejecting) the other two more central emphases. When we embrace this fuller understanding of shalom, all three focuses integrate into a single whole and produce peace.

I've also come to see how there is an intimate connection between shalom and salvation in the Old Testament. As shalom exposed the injustices of Israel's slavery in Egypt, so, too, is the concept of salvation most clearly reflected in their freedom from that bondage. The Hebrew word for salvation, *hoshia*, refers largely to liberation from political, social, and economic oppression and hardship, such as what God's people experienced in Egypt. A later variation of the word, *yesh'ua*, also deals exclusively with political, social, and economic injustice. Does this surprise you? Of all the places where *saved* is used in the

Old Testament, we could count on one hand the number of times it is used in reference to something "spiritual" or referring to issues of piety and righteousness (what we might call personal sin issues). The overwhelming use of the idea of salvation clearly places an emphasis on present freedom. This is important to understand, because when we look at Jesus's own use of the word *salvation*, this is the context from which He is speaking.

The foundations of shalom are tied indivisibly with the work of salvation God is doing in the world, here and now. When shalom shapes the saving work of God, it distinguishes itself from the justice we are so used to seeing in the world. The salvation of God is given, not to those who deserve it or who earn it, but to those who truly need it, whether they deserve it or not. Salvation is not a reward in some spiritual transaction, but the pure grace of God acting in loving compassion for those in need. Much of the suffering we see God's people experience in Scripture is self-inflicted, yet time and again God pursued them lovingly, calling them to repentance and *saving* them from their bondage. It does not mean that God withholds discipline, but His discipline is not retributive. Rather it is designed to point toward repentance. God's justice is restorative justice. In other words, the Jewish people were not liberated from Egypt because they were good; they were liberated from Egypt because God is good. Both shalom and salvation are motivated by the same thing: God's love.

Isn't it interesting to note that the Hebrew word for salvation shares the same root as the name Joshua? Joshua led God's people out of the wilderness and into the Promised Land. In Greek, the name Joshua is translated as Jesus—Jesus who leads His people out of the bondage to the fear of death and to death itself, and into His kingdom of shalom. The implications of this association are worthy of much consideration. This leads us naturally to the next question: what do shalom and salvation mean in the New Testament?

The word *shalom* is not used explicitly in the New Testament because it is written in the Greek, not Hebrew. However, given the Greek translation of the Old Testament, we can discern that when the Greek word *eirene* is used in the New Testament, usually translated as *peace*, it is safe to assume that it carries the same intention of meaning as *shalom*. *Eirene* is used in the New Testament largely in the same way *shalom* is used in the Old Testament, affirming the three general categories (and their emphases): physical/material well-being, social/relational harmony, and morality/ethics.

But when we reach Romans 15:33, we encounter something entirely new: "The God of peace be with all of you. Amen." Here, for the first time in all of Scripture, God is directly named as the God of shalom. The centrality of God's emphasis on shalom is becoming more and more clear to God's people. Because Jesus is the clearest revelation humanity has ever had of the nature and character of God, that shalom-nature must have been central to the example and teachings of Jesus Himself. And if shalom is central to the image of God, and we are created in God's image, then living into shalom is part of what it means for us to reflect and to be restored to God's image. It is not something simply required of us, but something that is to be descriptive of our nature.

LIVING FOR SHALOM

Surely *this* is what it means for us to be missional. Ephesians 6:15 explicitly ties shalom with the gospel itself: "As shoes for your feet put on whatever will make you ready to proclaim the gospel of peace." It is not hard to connect the imagery of shoes on our feet with the mission of God when we consider the journey St. Patrick undertook to return to live among the Irish.

Further, in Romans 5, we discover that the peace/shalom in our relationship with God is the result of the justification that comes through Jesus Christ. Yet, we must not miss the fact that Jesus does not die for the committed. He didn't make a sign-up sheet and say, "Listen, if you are interested in salvation, could you sign up here, please? I want to make sure that enough of you are on board before I commit to this."

Instead, Jesus embraced the costly sacrifice necessary to restore us to shalom "while we still were sinners," while we were enemies of God. If this is what Christ did for us, for the sake of shalom salvation and love while we were still His enemies—what does that tell us about what is required of us as His active Body who are to be going about His mission in the world? We've seen all of the necessary qualities of such a person in the fearless willingness of St. Patrick to face his pretense, hear what God wants of him, and then do it. This is the central witness to the love and grace of God, a witness we are called to live. This is what forms the "martyrological" identity of God's people and shaped the mission

St. Patrick led in Ireland. In this way, shalom in the New Testament is defined by what it is and does positively, not by what it is not or what it is against. Jesus demonstrates that shalom/peace is both the end we seek *and* the means by which we seek it. Shalom is at the heart of our mission, of our purpose, and of our very hope.

We have been trying to live this out here in community at Little Flowers. Together, we've studied this quotation from Perry Yoder:

> Is it not a major tragedy of the church that it has failed to fulfill either the hope of Hebrew Scriptures or the purposes of God in the atoning work of Christ for shalom? Will this not remain true until relationships within the Christian community which are now so fragmented along national and class lines are transformed? *If the coming of shalom demands a transformation, should not the church be leading the way in dismantling the structures of oppression and death wherever they are found so that shalom, God's will, may be done on earth as it is in heaven?*[40]

Throughout the Bible, we see these themes consistently, demonstrating that shalom is at the heart of the saving mission of God's people in the world. We are trying to be an integral part, in our small way, in the community where we live, of this shalom.

One of the most beautiful practices that encompass this idea is the tradition of the Love Feast. Often referred to as Agape meals, these shared, communal celebrations of Christians go back to the earliest of Church history, even suggested in the New Testament (1 Cor. 11). Love Feasts were rooted in the shared faith of believers and were tied closely to the practices of Eucharist. And while Love Feasts and the Eucharist developed distinct from one another over time, they have always been tied together on a fundamental level. Such communal meals of celebration were not a new thing when they emerged among the early Christians, since both Jewish and Gentile cultures had their own equivalents. However, it did not take much time for the Christian expression of these meals to distinguish themselves.

Perhaps the most unique characteristic of the early Christian Love Feast was how it was used to break down barriers by bringing people together. Because the early Christians believed they were united by the Spirit as one family—that there was "no longer Jew or Greek," "no longer slave or free," and "no longer male and female; for all of you are one in Christ Jesus" (Gal. 3:28)—the social, economic, and religious barriers (to name a few) were defied, subverted, and even done away with. I know that sounds like a lot—but they were also just shared meals.

These meals would see men and women gathering with the intimacy reserved for family members alone. Rich and poor dined together, with no preference given to those of privilege (as the Epistle of James so clearly reflects). Even slaves and their masters would come together as sister and brother before Christ to remember and celebrate what Jesus had accomplished to bring them together.

This may sound like a noble and romantic reality, but it was actually a difficult task for the early believers. They were constantly confronted with their own pride, fear, and shame. The constructs of the outsiders—women, the poor, the slave, the sick, the Gentile—were being dismantled, confronting them with their own bondage to systems caught up in fear and self-service. Again, the Epistle of James demonstrates that this commitment to breaking down barriers in worship was often resisted and needed reinforcing. The writer challenges the believers to stop showing favoritism toward the rich (Jas. 2:1–7), defending the need to encounter all in the next verse (8) by reminding them: "You do well if you really fulfill the royal law according to the scripture, 'You shall love your neighbor as yourself.'" Such a command was not mere housekeeping but went to the very heart of Jesus's own summation of all the law and all the prophets:

> He said to him, "You shall love the Lord your God with all your heart, and with all your soul, and with all your mind." This is the greatest and first commandment. And a second is like it: "You shall love your neighbor as yourself." On these two commandments hang all the law and the prophets. (Matt. 22:37–40)

Rooted, as they were, on this fundamental truth of the gospel, these choices would stand as subversive protests against the principalities and powers of the surrounding world. Outsiders would view these Christians as dangerous, too accepting and welcoming, scandalous and compromised. It is not surprising, then, that the powers that be quickly turned their attention to crushing this movement. Their appeal among "the least of these" who were joining them, adding to their number daily, was a threat to their control and perceived stability. For these reasons the Love Feast became—and still does become—a powerful icon for shalom.

When St. Patrick returned to Ireland, he did not hide his history as a slave among them. Suddenly, he found himself at the table with his former captors, breaking bread and sharing the cup. How was this possible? Consider this: nowhere in Scripture is slavery explicitly condemned. In some places, in fact, it seems accepted as the norm, if not even explicitly affirmed. But today, I can think of no Christians who stand up in support of slavery. We universally denounce it as evil, right? Well, how did this happen? Did we simply become more enlightened, embracing a more progressive view than the Bible? Far from it!

The seeds of the end of slavery can be found in these simple Agape meals. Imagine the scenario: if masters and slaves, who were both Christians, came together to share these meals as brothers and sisters, equally served by the other in genuine mutuality, how long do you think that relationship of master and slave could last? How long could we exploit the labor and lives of our family, our fellow members in the Body of Christ? So the seeds of the end of slavery were planted, in the same way that many other barriers that divide us began to crumble—barriers of race, gender, nationality, religion, sexual orientation, and more. So shalom began to emerge.

While we do need to address the larger, global issues of injustice and seek shalom there as well, we could also do better trusting the example of Jesus who demonstrated that faithfully embracing love right where we are at can turn the course of empires. This is how someone like St. Francis of Assisi, who did not seek to create a massive order of power and influence, could produce a movement that to this day is changing the world. This is why St. Patrick's mission transformed not only a nation, but laid the seeds to save much of Western civilization, just as so many other Christians have done throughout history.

In 1942, centuries after St. Patrick left for Ireland and over twenty years before Martin Luther King Jr.'s historic "I Have a Dream" speech, two Christian couples decided to found an alternative community in the heart of the American South amid systemic and violent racism and prejudice. On a 440-acre plot of land near Americus, Georgia, they formed an interracial, intentional Christian community farm where blacks and whites would live and work together as equals. While this might sound less than radical to our current sensibilities, for that time and in that place it was completely unheard of and extremely dangerous for all involved. That community was called Koinonia (κοινωνία), for the Greek word for *fellowship* or *communion*.

The members of Koinonia Farm seemed to understand the significance of living an alternative politic of reconciliation around the four fundamental relationships in a world that not only vilified their efforts, but in some cases criminalized it. Regardless of race, every member of this decidedly nonviolent community was considered absolutely equal in all things, even going so far as to share their possessions in common. Even by today's standards, such a radical example of living out the kingdom on earth as it is heaven is hard to find. In that era, it began to create resentment, anger, and even outright hatred, spurred on by the growing controversy of the emerging civil rights movement. As a result, the community faced social alienation, commercial boycotting, and even violent attacks, including several bombings.

Amid all of these threats to their livelihoods and lives, the founders of Koinonia Farm remained committed to their calling of being a community of radical equality, simplicity, and love in a world of hate. This is not to say it was easy. While every member of the community was committed to their vision and values, no one was completely free of their own prejudices, privilege, and painful histories. The internal challenge of sustaining such a community was taxing and difficult, let alone the forces on the outside that were bent on trying to destroy them. But they prevailed, transformed by their struggles, both internal and external. To this day Koinonia Partners remains a place of radical welcome, reconciliation, and hopeful possibility to the world. While often forgotten in the annals of the civil rights era, the powerful witness and impact of this group of people stretches from the quiet country roads of rural Georgia to the Oval Office and hearts of American presidents.

In our small church, Little Flowers Community, we gather every Sunday evening around a shared potluck meal where all are welcome. The people who join us are very different from each other in many ways, people who would not often find themselves in each other's company, let alone gathered together for Christian worship. It can be messy, at times, both physically and socially, but it is also deeply beautiful as we share real life with one another. And while we still practice a more formal Eucharist at times, that meal is our communion, an open table to welcome all into the reconciliation that God promises, offering fullness of life to every individual and the hope of shalom for all creation.

Costly Faithfulness
From Being Jesus to Seeing Jesus

had just fallen asleep around midnight when the
phone rang, startling me into groggy wakefulness. The
call display showed the name of a neighbor and friend
who was the landlord of the building Alan had moved into
when he separated from Beth. Rubbing my eyes, I mumbled
a confused greeting into the phone. But what I heard next
snapped me immediately awake, my heart racing:

"Alan's dead!"

Stunned, I asked the person to repeat himself.

"Alan's dead. His roommates just found him in his room.
The ambulance and police are on their way."

Shaken to the core, with no time to consider other
possibilities, I quickly dressed and, along with a friend, ran

up the street to Beth's home to tell her the devastating news. Holding her as she wept, we felt the unbearable burden of grief and sadness.

Hours later, after a long night of waiting and wondering, we learned that Alan's death was, in fact, a result of natural causes—a seemingly random series of events that no one could have predicted or prevented. While we took some small comfort in the knowledge that he had not ended his own life, his death was no less final. Then there were so many unanswered questions, so many unresolved wounds. There were so many unsaid words of love and forgiveness. How could death be said to have no sting when we faced such painful loss?

WE RETURN TO DEATH—AND DESTROY IT

Facing death and the fear it instills in us, we know that these paradoxical questions are not contradictions. Indeed, we have great faith that Christ has conquered death, not only freeing us from the bondage of fear it creates, but also promising that we will one day be reunited with those whom death has taken from us. At the same time, though, we recognize that death as we know it was never God's intention for His creatures or creation. It is a disruption amid the peace, joy, and love He intended. So, to feel that pain and mourn that loss is to give witness to what shouldn't be and lends gravity to the hope we embrace.

When Jesus learned of the death of his friend Lazarus, the gospels reveal what an appropriate response to death might look like when it says, "Jesus wept." Jesus felt the pain of grief and loss. We take great comfort in knowing that God's loving heart grieves for the pain of loss that comes with death. God is not distant or impassive to the pain and confusion we are left with, but is a real and present Comforter among us.

We will never know the outcome of Beth and Alan's work toward reconciliation. While Alan was committed to making things right and striving toward that end, he was also still living in the bondage that led him to his poor choices to begin with. This can feel hopeless to those of us left behind. Yet, we also know that death and its sting have been ultimately defeated. In the light of that hope, we can stand with Christ, remembering His words when He promised: "Blessed are those who mourn, for they will be comforted."

Liberty from the fear of death does not mean we will never face death ourselves. Like St. Patrick and Alan, we all face our inevitable mortality. Yet, the freedom from fear allows us to face death with a posture no longer ruled by self-preservation. At the beginning of this book I included the following quote by Craig Hovey: "The virtues necessary to be a martyr are no different from the virtues necessary to be a faithful Christian."[41] When I first read this quote, it sounded strange and dark to me. It used terminology familiar enough, but when I considered its meaning, the sentence seemed overstated, even impossible. There seemed to be a vast chasm between its meaning and my experience. How could I possibly know what it means to be a martyr? The martyrs seem to be so exceptionally heroic that I could not possibly hope to count myself among them.

Now I realize that real martyrs, both living and dead, are heroic, but not in the ways we might expect. Their lives are not simply characterized by an absence of fear, but by a liberty from their fear. Through the transformation that we have seen in Scripture and illustrated through the life of St. Patrick, they possess a freedom from the bondage of the fear of death that, by the Holy Spirit, empowers them to face the end of human life so heroically. It is as we discover their humble humanity that we come to accept our own. When we see in them the all-too-human idiosyncrasies and imperfections of human experience, we find hope that we, too, can share in the same freedom that allowed them to so faithfully love and serve God and others.

The hope for that liberty is found when we are willing to embrace the vulnerable faith of St. Patrick and expose our brokenness and need without excuse or recourse.

Vulnerability such as this might once have represented a threat to us. But I pray that we now can see how such openness is the opportunity to find fullness of life as faithful followers of Jesus. Gone is the impulse to settle for a mediocre religious devotion that merely seeks to appease the unspoken status quo of faithfulness. We have been presented with the thrilling miracle of resurrection life, discovering that our brokenness, through Christ, can become a means to demonstrate His love and hope to others. In this way we can truly believe that when, "I am weak, then I am strong" (2 Cor. 12:10).

Vulnerability. By definition, we are frightened of it. By instinct, we do all we can to avoid it. This is why so many Christians miss the depth and wisdom in the twelve steps. Viewed as necessary therapeutic treatment for extreme cases of chemical addiction, we fail to see that the freedom often discovered by people in recovery is rooted in a (paradoxically powerful) vulnerable faith. They begin with their common weakness, their brokenness, and their unequivocal need for the intervention of a power beyond their means. Christians might recognize, too, that we begin the process of redemption with our common weaknesses and brokenness, and only then can we truly understand what is necessary to be strong (in our weakness) and wise (in our foolishness). At other times we call this taking up our cross and dying to self to follow Jesus.

Few of us will ever face the real threat of genuine martyrdom, but the fear of the consequences of embracing this kind of vulnerable faith will be enough to make us second-guess such serious commitments. Only by the power and love of the Holy Spirit, in the midst of a loving and mutually vulnerable community of faith, can we face these fears, trusting God to do in us the impossible work of making us into His ordinary saints who live with extraordinary love.

The process of writing this book throughout the past year has forced me to face my own fears and selfish motivations, confronted by the tragedy of Alan's death and all that preceded it. In so doing, I have begun to more deeply understand the simple, profound calling of a truly vulnerable faith. As you engage these simple truths, you, too, will begin to encounter this transformation—that is, you will probably see that the most defining characteristic of a martyr is not that they were killed or even willing to die. They were simply free enough to embrace a faithfulness to Jesus unhindered by the bondage of fear, shame, and selfishness. They were free enough to love.

What would I do for Alan if he were alive today? I am not certain. But I would listen, I would love him, and I would support him. I would be vulnerable with Alan in ways that I'm only just beginning to understand.

We are all on a journey of transformation. St. Patrick was on such a journey, as we've seen, and each stage drew him deeper into the redemptive work of Christ to make him a new creation. As that creation slowly emerged, the transformation became the seed by which millions of others encountered the love of God and His shalom kingdom. Each of us in our vulnerable faith can be a missional people about God's work in the world. We become His witnesses—His *martos*—to our neighbors across the street and to the ends of the earth.

Above all is the centrality of love at the heart of vulnerable faith. Vulnerability will thrive only where love abounds—a love that is generous, gracious, patient, compassionate, humble, curious, joyful, and full of hope. In the absence of fear and the bondage it inflicts on us, love will put down roots, grow, and extend its reach far beyond our expectations or natural capacity. Love we once reserved only for those closest to us can be offered even to those who would persecute us. Enemies are transformed into sisters and brothers and friends. Living out this love is the missional life in the radical way of St. Patrick, in the radical way of Jesus. It is all that I desire.

St. Patrick's Breastplate

We bind ourselves today to the strong virtue of love,
In the invocation of the Trinity, in the Threeness,
Confessing the Oneness of the Creator.

We bind ourselves today to the virtue of Christ's birth and with
His baptism,
To the virtue of His death and His burial in the tomb,
To the virtue of His resurrection, His ascension, and the sending
of His Spirit,
And to the virtue of His promised return.

We bind ourselves today to the virtue of Heaven,
In the brightness of Sun,
In the whiteness of Snow,
In the radiance of Fire,
In the flash of Lightning,
In the sweeping of Wind,
In the depth of Sea,
In the stability of Earth,
In the denseness of Rock.

We bind ourselves today, God's virtue to guide us,

God's strength to uphold us,

God's wisdom to inform us,

God's eye to see before us,

God's ear to listen to us,

God's Word to speak to us,

God's hand to hold us,

God's way set before us,

God's shield to guard us,

God's host to secure us,

Against snares of fear,

Against seductions of selfishness,

Against any who would harm us,

Both near and far,

The one or the many.

Christ with us, Christ before us, Christ behind us, Christ in us.

Christ below us and above us.

Christ to our right, Christ to our left.

Christ in breadth, in length, in height, and in depth.

Christ in the heart of everyone who thinks of us,

Christ in the mouth of everyone who speaks to us,

Christ in every eye that sees us,

Christ in every ear that hears us.

We bind ourselves today to the strong virtue of love,

In the invocation of the Trinity, in the Threeness,

Confessing the Oneness of the Creator.

Salvation is the Father's, salvation is the Son's,

salvation is Spirit's.

Your salvation, O Lord, always be with us.

Amen.[42]

NOTES

1   Craig Hovey, *To Share in the Body: A Theology of Martyrdom for Today's Church* (Grand Rapids, MI: Brazos Press, 2008), 60.

2   See http://www.catholicnewsagency.com/news/catholics-are-called-to-daily-martyrdom-says-pope/.

3   Ibid.

4   Dietrich Bonhoeffer, *The Cost of Discipleship* (New York: Touchstone, 1995), 43.

5   See http://en.wikipedia.org/wiki/Twelve-step_program#Twelve_Steps.

6   For a full treatment on the Beatitudes, please see my book *The Cost of Community: Jesus, St. Francis & Life in the Kingdom* (Downers Grove, IL: InterVarsity Press, 2011).

7   See http://www.drphil.com/articles/article/44.

8   Richard Beck, *Slavery of Death* (Eugene, OR: Wipf & Stock, 2013), 8.

9   This thesis is powerfully demonstrated in the Pulitzer Prize–winning book *Denial of Death* by Ernest Becker (New York: Free Press, 1997).

10   M. Scott Peck, *The Different Drum* (New York: Touchstone, 1998), 88.

11   For more on this idea of being "cracked Eikons," see Scot McKnight's excellent book *Embracing Grace* (Brewster, MA: Paraclete Press, 2012).

12   See http://en.wikipedia.org/wiki/Twelve-step_program#Twelve_Steps.

13   M. Scott Peck, *The Different Drum* (New York: Touchstone, 1998), 90.

14   Richard Beck, *Slavery of Death* (Eugene, OR: Wipf & Stock, 2013), xi.

15   Bruce L. Shelley, *Church History in Plain Language: Fourth Edition* (Nashville, TN: Thomas Nelson, 2012), 38.

16   See http://en.wikipedia.org/wiki/Twelve-step_program#Twelve_Steps.

17   Step 5, http://en.wikipedia.org/wiki/Twelve-step_program#Twelve_Steps.

18   Terence T. Gorski, *Fireside; Reissue Edition* (New York: April 15, 1991).

19   See http://en.wikipedia.org/wiki/Twelve-step_program#Twelve_Steps.

20   *Instinct*, directed by Jon Turteltaub, (Los Angeles: Spyglass Entertainment, 1999), film.

21   Richard Beck, *Slavery of Death* (Eugene, OR: Wipf & Stock, 2013), 59.

22   Ibid., 70.

23   Ibid., 77.

24   Ibid.

25 Dietrich Bonhoeffer, *Life Together* (New York: Harper & Row, 1954), 30.

26 From http://postsecretdotcom.files.wordpress.com/2014/03/6-11-2years.jpg.

27 From http://postsecretdotcom.files.wordpress.com/2014/03/first.jpg.

28 From http://postsecretdotcom.files.wordpress.com/2014/03/1-ring.jpg.

29 M. Scott Peck, *The Different Drum* (New York: Touchstone, 1998), 65.

30 *The Confession of Saint Patrick and Letter to Coroticus*, 1st ed. (New York, NY: Image, 1998), 23.

31 Dietrich Bonhoeffer, *Life Together* (New York: Harper & Row, 1954), 17.

32 While the history between Christian traditions has not always been characterized by love and grace, I am encouraged that the work of reconciliation within the broader Christian traditions continues. I am particularly appreciative of the relationship and reconciliation found between Mennonites and Catholics through the Bridgefolk movement. Bridgefolk is "a movement of sacramentally-minded Mennonites and peace-minded Roman Catholics who come together to celebrate each other's traditions, explore each other's practices, and honor each other's contribution to the mission of Christ's Church" (http://www.bridgefolk.net/).

33 For a beautiful exploration of the witness of repentance, see Mark Van Steenwyk's *The Unkingdom of God: Embracing the Subversive Power of Repentance* (Downers Grove, IL: InterVarsity Press, 2013).

34 See http://en.wikipedia.org/wiki/Twelve-step_program#Twelve_Steps.

35 Jean Vanier, *Community and Growth* (Mahwah, NJ: Paulist Press, 1989), 82.

36 While I have learned from several sources on the topic of *shalom*, I am especially indebted to the work of Perry Yoder, namely his book *Shalom: The Bible's Word for Peace, Justice & Salvation* (Nappanee, IN: Evangel Publishing House, 1998).

37 Walter Brueggemann, *Peace: Living Toward a Vision* (St. Louis: Chalice Press, 2001), 51.

38 Randy Woodley, *Shalom and the Community of Creation* (Grand Rapids, MI: Wm. B. Eerdmans, 2012), 25.

39 John Driver, *Kingdom Citizens* (Scottdale, PA: Herald Press, 1980),65.

40 Perry Yoder, *Shalom: The Bible's Word for Peace, Justice & Salvation* (Nappanee, IN: Evangel Publishing House, 1998), 23. I owe most of the insights in this chapter to Yoder's essential work here.

41 Craig Hovey, *To Share in the Body: A Theology of Martyrdom for Today's Church* (Grand Rapids, MI: Brazos Press, 2008), 60.

42 Adapted from St. Patrick's Breastplate by the author.

ABOUT PARACLETE PRESS

WHO WE ARE

Paraclete Press is a publisher of books, recordings, and DVDs on Christian spirituality. Our publishing represents a full expression of Christian belief and practice—from Catholic to Evangelical, from Protestant to Orthodox.

We are the publishing arm of the Community of Jesus, an ecumenical monastic community in the Benedictine tradition. As such, we are uniquely positioned in the marketplace without connection to a large corporation and with informal relationships to many branches and denominations of faith.

WHAT WE ARE DOING

Paraclete Press Books Paraclete publishes books that show the richness and depth of what it means to be Christian. Although Benedictine spirituality is at the heart of all that we do, we publish books that reflect the Christian experience across many cultures, time periods, and houses of worship. We publish books that nourish the vibrant life of the church and its people.

We have several different series, including the best-selling Paraclete Essentials and Paraclete Giants series of classic texts in contemporary English; Voices from the Monastery—men and women monastics writing about living a spiritual life today; award-winning poetry; best-selling gift books for children on the occasions of baptism and First Communion; and the Active Prayer Series that brings creativity and liveliness to any life of prayer.

Mount Tabor Books Paraclete's newest series, Mount Tabor Books, focuses on liturgical worship, art and art history, ecumenism, and the first-millennium church; and it was created in conjunction with the Mount Tabor Ecumenical Centre for Art and Spirituality in Barga, Italy.

Paraclete Recordings From Gregorian chant to contemporary American choral works, our recordings celebrate the best of sacred choral music composed through the centuries that create a space for heaven and earth to intersect. Paraclete Recordings is the record label representing the internationally acclaimed choir Gloriæ Dei Cantores, praised for their "rapt and fathomless spiritual intensity" by *American Record Guide*; the Gloriæ Dei Cantores Schola, specializing in the study and performance of Gregorian chant; and the other instrumental artists of the Gloriæ Dei Artes Foundation.

Paraclete Press is also privileged to be the exclusive North American distributor of the recordings of the Monastic Choir of St. Peter's Abbey in Solesmes, France, long considered to be a leading authority on Gregorian chant.

Paraclete Video Our DVDs offer spiritual help, healing, and biblical guidance for a broad range of life issues including grief and loss, marriage, forgiveness, facing death, bullying, addictions, Alzheimer's, and spiritual formation.

Learn more about us at our website www.paracletepress.com or phone us toll-free at 1.800.451.500

SCAN TO READ MORE

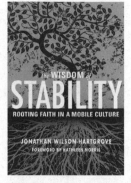

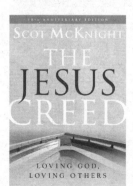